I Didn't Do It Alone

I Didn't Do It Alone

The Autobiography of
Art Linkletter

As told to George Bishop

Caroline House Publishers, Inc.
Ottawa, Illinois & Ossining, New York

Copies of this book may be purchased from the publisher for $10.95. All inquiries and catalog requests should be addressed to Caroline House Publishers, Inc., Box 738, Ottawa, Illinois 61350 — (815) 434-7905.

ISBN: 0-89803-040-4

LIBRARY OF CONGRESS

CATALOG CARD NO.: 80-67455

    Bishop, George & Linkletter, Art
      I didn't do it alone.
    Ottawa, Ill: Caroline House Publishers
    220 p.
8010   800630

Prologue

The ominous midsummer storm clouds hanging low over Walla Walla, Washington, reflected the mood of the country in early 1929. Unemployment ran high and would go higher in the months following the October 24 stock market collapse that plunged our nation into a dreadful depression.

However, the coming local and national storms meant little to a group of men assembled on the outskirts of Walla Walla not far from the confluence of the Walla Walla and Mill Creek rivers, whose fast flowing waters fed lumber and agricultural products into the thriving town just north of the Oregon border. Walla Walla was thriving in the midst of an economic slowdown because it was a key railway division point in the days when the nation's commercial lifelines consisted of thousands of miles of parallel steel rails crisscrossing the forty-eight states.

Long freight and passenger trains of the Chicago, Milwaukee,

St. Paul, and Pacific railroad crossed the Idaho line to be routed northwest to Seattle and on up the Pacific Coast to British Columbia or almost due west to Portland, then south toward California. Spokane, queen of the Inland Empire, sent timber, ore, and grain into Walla Walla for distribution to points west and south through rail yards large enough to service a city many times its size.

Folks did not usually travel to Walla Walla for extended visits; it was a town to live in or pass through, and it was this second option that appealed to the twenty or so men sitting around an open fire under a railroad culvert just beyond the switching yard. They included an attorney, a medical student, a bricklayer, a butcher, and a stranded circus roustabout; also present were men who were running from the law, and a few professional wanderers. All, as they sat watching some slumgullion bubble appetizingly in a giant metal pot, had two things in common: they were down on their luck and they were hoboes, whose goals grew more vague as their time on the bum lengthened. They were not godless men; for the most part, they were drifters who, because of circumstances and their own folly, in their despair had temporarily lost touch with their Maker.

There were a lot of men on the road and riding the rails in those days, and their numbers would soon increase. A common bond quickly developed among them; they were, for the most part, peaceful and mutually helpful. Bums walking into a hobo jungle were welcome for they brought news of friendly or tough towns, the traffic flow through other division points across the country, and, most important, the state of mind of the railroad detectives, called bulls, toward nonpaying transients in their domains.

Two late arrivals, hurrying to escape the start of a heavy downpour, were scarcely noticed as, each hanging on to his belongings wrapped in a small canvas sack strung over one shoulder with a rough cord, they scrambled down the bank and thankfully took their places under the shelter of the culvert's overhang.

The two new hoboes appeared slightly younger than the others. One, slim and wiry, had been baptized Denver Colorado Fox, right out of a story by Mark Twain. Fox's companion was bigger-boned and taller, with fairish hair; his name was Art Linkletter.

Chapter One

Today, many young people faced with my very limited choices back in 1929 often "turn off and drop out," wallowing in a spaced-out self-pity that blames everyone but themselves for real or imagined misfortunes. True, things were simpler in those days. And, yes, I knew young men who failed to meet the challenge and ended up drunk, in jail, or, as the depression worsened, dead by their own hands. But most of us with no fixed goals in life took a positive approach; we went searching for a solution.

In well-heeled families they called that search "traveling to improve oneself." In the Linkletter social strata it was called "riding the rails." Although the objectives and methods of transportation were the same, the whole concept lost something in the translation.

My adoptive father, John Linkletter, couldn't give me the money to travel in style but he gave me something else that a brash young boy of sixteen didn't appreciate at the time: his faith. And I believe now that it helped take me farther than any first-class ticket and, often without my realizing it, shielded and comforted me in times of trouble.

I was always a self-reliant person, sure that my wits and presence of mind would get me out of any tough situation. Lately, though, now that I have more money than I ever dreamed of, I remember I started out with a life goal of earning three hundred dollars a month.

My mettle was early tested in that Walla Walla switching yard and, although I thought at the time that only chance prevented Denver's and my death, as I look back on it I think we had a little help from another source.

We were tired from the long trek up the coast from San Diego. After listening to the old-timers lecture on the state of the Union Pacific at various division points, we took the advice of a hobo I remember only as a recently displaced New York stockbroker. He said the Chicago, Milwaukee, St. Paul, and Pacific offered the choicest accommodations for our proposed trip. We wanted to head for the big cities so we walked along the sidings until we found several cars that were part of a train being made up for the run east.

Now freight trains are not the best way to travel on the bum. They are constantly being shunted onto sidings so that one or several cars can be detached for local delivery. The twin inconveniences of very slow passage and the danger of ending up in some small town that hates hoboes, hundreds of miles off your path, make the freights second-class travel for the knights of the road.

But Denver and I were beginners and we had learned that slow and uncertain though the freights might be, they were also relatively safe and easy. Many a bum had died before his time because he was either too impatient or too stupid to serve a freight-train apprenticeship and opted for the luxury—and hazards—of a "blind baggage" perch on a fast passenger special.

This night, bone weary and drenched by a summertime Washington downpour, we were more than happy to locate a dry, loaded freight car, climb atop the cargo, and, after checking to see if we had company, take off our wet shoes and settle down for some much needed sleep.

That was another survival rule of the road. Never get into a car with one or two strangers, or a whole lot of bums who obviously are riding as a group. In either case you had no way of knowing the intentions of your fellow passengers, of knowing whether they were armed, or whether they made their way by preying on young or simply incautious novices.

Empty cars were a good way to travel though not, we soon learned, the most interesting. Ideally, I would watch for a car that had several hoboes in it who had climbed aboard separately. There was real safety in numbers in that situation and the conversations and card games made the miles and hours slip by quickly. As the depression worsened, the quality of hoboes continued to improve; often professional men traveled with us and many a night I've drifted off to sleep too tired to keep listening to a heated argument on the place of woman's suffrage in the trade-union movement. Come to think of it, I heard that very same discussion repeated in the White House dining room during a recent visit to Washington at the invitation of the President to address House and Senate leaders on the drug problem. Could be some of them had been involved in our boxcar seminars.

Does that sound farfetched? Perhaps you've heard of Le Bistro, the ultraexclusive Beverly Hills supper club that caters to the famous and wealthy. Not everyone can reserve a table at Le Bistro and, human nature being what it is, that makes it all the more desirable. Although I am not a partygoer any more—I'm not much of a drinker and the small talk is a bore—I went to a small, intimate gathering at Le Bistro because some good friends were going to be there.

After dinner, over coffee and liqueurs, I found myself engaged in deep conversation with H. L. Hunt, the noted financier and philanthropist. So intense was our discussion that we quite unwittingly excluded the rest of our table, prompting one of the guests, I think it was the beautiful dancing star Ann Miller, to ask kiddingly what weighty matters of politics or high finance so completely held our attention.

I feel that I break no confidences to reveal that Hunt and Linkletter were swapping experiences when they were both on the road, as hoboes. When I was riding the rails up north I had heard stories around the jungle campfires about the exploits of legendary bums and the name Arizona Slim more than once crept into the conversation. Not until that evening at Le Bistro did I learn that Arizona Slim and H. L. Hunt were one and the same! And we *were* discussing high finance that evening in Beverly Hills. We were both marveling at the irony in the fact that in the hobo jungles of our youths we found mostly cooperation and camaraderie, whereas in the jungles of high finance to which we had both "graduated" we very often encountered a cynical struggle for advantage.

H. L. Hunt's recollections confirmed my own: most of our experiences traveling across the country and in other parts of the world as hoboes were good. And I believe that I stayed out of serious trouble because both Denver and I were on our guard; very likely Someone was watching over us as well.

We had no sooner settled down when the pitch black of the car interior was pierced by the flare from a match. We lay motionless, watching two dirty and unshaven bums climb the packing crates that reached almost to the ceiling. The match went out and another was lighted as they crawled toward us on their hands and knees. They had seen us come in and were up to no good. If they had wanted merely to ride they would have turned away from us and gone to the other end of the car.

Scarcely a foot away another match revealed that the second man was holding a revolver pointed straight at us.

"Put your hands straight out and lie flat," he ordered. "If I hear anything move when the match goes out I'll shoot."

As he searched our pockets and felt around our middles I wondered if money was all they wanted. I was frightened and I could hear Denver breathing too quickly near me. We had both heard stories of older hoboes attacking young boys sexually and I knew real fear for the first time. The match went out, was relighted, and we didn't move. He found a dollar and thirty cents on me but missed ten dollars I had sewn into my coat lining; he took two dollars that Denver had in one pocket.

The match went out and I could tell by their manner that they were undecided about something. At first I thought it was because they hadn't found enough money to suit them, but gradually the truth dawned on me and sent a cold chill down my back. We lay there, face to face, inches apart in the darkness and I heard the hammer click back on the gun. I had never heard that sound before but I'll never forget it. We had seen their faces and they were thinking—or at least the gunman was thinking—of killing us.

There was little risk for them. Not only would the rain that hammered down on the boxcar drown any noise, but we were so far down the yard that no one could hear the shots anyway—not that anybody would have come to investigate; hoboes learn early to mind their own business.

So we lay there and I thought of my father and how he would have prayed for me had he known. Strange, but that is how I thought; not that *I* was praying but how he would have prayed. Suddenly the fear left me. I remember it as though a protective blanket had been pulled over me. One instant my muscles were tensed, waiting for I knew not what, then suddenly there were only peace and calm in the darkness around me. It was as though a presence had made itself felt and assured me that all would be well.

Seconds later I heard them starting to move back. One of

them, the match holder I think, pushed something over until it touched my arm.

"Here's your thirty cents," he said. "Breakfast money."

And then they left. One minute they were considering killing us, I felt certain of that, and the next they left us enough money to eat. They had been drinking; I could smell liquor on their breaths. So maybe that was it, alcohol dulls the senses and makes people behave irrationally. That's what Denver thought and I said nothing about my feelings because I was afraid he would laugh. Perhaps in thinking of my father's prayers I had unknowingly prayed, and at least now I feel that those prayers were answered.

Back then I had no time for philosophical reflection. In the darkness of that freight car as the train rolled east across the great northern states I could think only of our narrow escape and wonder if perhaps I had been too hasty in deciding to leave San Diego and strike out on my own. But even then, with the memory of that gun still fresh in my mind, my resolve never really weakened, because the truth was that I wanted to be separated from the two most kindly people I had ever known, John and Mary Linkletter. They had adopted me when I was a baby, given up by my unmarried mother Effie Brown in Moose Jaw, a small town near Regina, the capital of Canada's Saskatchewan province.

I was grateful to the Linkletters and remain grateful to this day; but gratitude wears thin in a sixteen-year-old anxious to make his way in the world and feeling, rightly or wrongly, that his father—I never speak of him as my adoptive father—was holding him back. I suppose, especially in this age of instant maturity, a lot of youngsters think that their parents are squares who fail to understand the allegedly profound message that they are trying to communicate, but with me it was a little different. I'm not particularly proud of the fact that my father embarrassed me, that at times I was ashamed to be seen with him, and that, in my heart of hearts, I felt he was something of an oddball.

Harsh words from the man who has entertained millions by being a nice guy? I suppose some of today's teenagers, those who can read, will take delight in having their own judgments confirmed by this symbol of American parenthood. "They have sown the wind and they shall reap the whirlwind." I know the sting of being criticized by those you love. In the first emotional reaction to my daughter Diane's death, some of my own children wondered aloud if I couldn't have done more to prevent it. Perhaps their disapproval, which happily they now understand was unwarranted, was the Almighty's way of reminding me that unwittingly I may have hurt a well-meaning old man back there in San Diego when I shrank from his company and took off on my own.

Fresh adventure awaited Denver and me as our freight rolled into Missoula, Montana, a main division point for the CMS & P. Rumors were flying thick and fast of trouble ahead and, the young mind being wonderfully adaptive, all thoughts of guilt and home quickly vanished. Our excitement spiced with rising apprehension, we watched our single track become two and then, magically beneath the wheels of the rushing freight, multiply into ten, twenty, and thirty or more sidings until we rolled to a stop.

Usually, in a switching yard most of the hoboes would either get off to stretch their legs or merely sit out the wait until cars had been shunted off and the main journey resumed. In Missoula everyone got off right away and headed into the surrounding woods or made for the local jungle. I soon learned why. A railroad bull nicknamed "Big Stick" had declared open war on unpaid passengers riding through his realm. He was bad news to us hoboes.

I was astounded to see more than a hundred men in the local jungle and heard there were twice as many camped out in the woods. As more trains arrived from all directions, the bums immediately got off and made themselves scarce, so esteemed was Big Stick's prowess.

The situation became critical. The small town of Missoula, never very friendly to begin with, could not possibly support a growing army of nearly four hundred hoboes. But that didn't bother Big Stick. He and a couple of his goons systematically worked the length of every train, whacking backs and heads of bums who were slow to respond.

Many of us younger, inexperienced hoboes were worried about rumors of vigilante action by the town's understandably upset residents. But the older fellows there, the only true professionals among men of many professions, refused to panic. They called a council of war in the jungle and one old guy, his seedy cutaway and army forage cap a seeming caricature of himself, allowed as how he had encountered a similar situation in Texas in the early twenties.

The old bum then explained what most of us knew: when a long, loaded freight gets up steam and starts rolling the engineer will not stop it for anything less than a major catastrophe. The plan for our liberation was simple, and I'll never forget what happened. Next morning, at dawn, as the mighty engines hissed and snorted into action, between three and four hundred hoboes, stretched as far as I could see, suddenly appeared, standing at intervals along both sides of the track. Big Stick and his goons were on patrol but they never expected anything like this.

The freight started moving and all of us ran alongside and swarmed aboard like pirates taking a treasure ship. Big Stick, snarling and cursing, managed to whack off a few, but as the train picked up speed he had to jump off. It was quite a sight—and good to be rolling eastward once again.

The Linkletter family's odyssey was also eastward, at first. My father sold insurance in Moose Jaw; rather, I should say he *didn't* sell insurance in Moose Jaw. So he and Mother decided, for reasons unknown to me, to open a small general store in Lowell, Massachusetts. There my dad displayed the same lack of business acumen, so off we went again, this time clear across the continent to settle in Point Fermin, near San Pedro, a Pacific port serving Los Angeles.

John Linkletter, searching for a way to feed the three of us, soon decided to move to more populous San Diego and resume the shoemaker's trade he had learned as a boy. We had no money and first had to live in a charity home run by a local church—a humiliating experience that registered strongly with a seven-year-old. I believe it was then I decided that I would, some day, earn the astronomical salary of three hundred dollars a month and with it assure myself and my parents of financial security for the remainder of our lives. Well, I have done that, but it took a little more than the three hundred.

My father opened a cobbler shop and, to my mother's pleased surprise, prospered at his trade. But our deliverance was also our undoing. The church had given us shelter and John Linkletter, a grateful and impressionable man, heard the call to the Lord's service. Which was all right, except that you cannot sew soles and save souls at the same time. Whenever Dad got a few dollars ahead he set out to preach the gospel. Those who listened to his formidable voice and expressed a desire to come forward were promptly invited home to dinner, making our house a popular if somewhat chaotic port of call.

The Reverend Mr. Linkletter, as he dubbed himself without going through any of the educational formalities, believed in the direct approach. Often I remember sitting with him on a bus when he spied someone obviously downcast over a pressing problem. My father would go over to him, introduce himself, and, in his best oratorical manner and offering his assistance, urge the man to seek the Lord's guidance. I was embarrassed by what I felt was his eccentric behavior and became resentful when we had to share our meager fare with strangers, many of whom were derelicts taking advantage of a good thing.

He would press me into service to provide entertainment in support of his street-corner preaching. Many a time the Reverend Mr. Linkletter, assisted by two brethren on cornet and tambourine and a future television star playing a shaky triangle, would exhort passersby to see the light.

When Dad Linkletter embraced the Four Square Pentecostal Church I was expected to show the proper religious fervor. Numerous times I have marched down the aisle, with hands raised and yelling the praises of the Lord, to bear witness to the fire of conversion burning in my veins. I have ducked countless pieces of flying crutches, smashed over nearby chairs to the accompaniment of stentorian testimony in tongues of the Lord's healing intervention.

My father's selfless dedication and what seemed to me other people's equally selfish capitalizing on his good instincts had a lot to do with the reputation for hardheaded materialism that quite justly followed my climb up the entertainment ladder. Other, more personal experiences in the early days helped too.

Since we were always stuck for money I took to doing odd jobs. One particular lady asked me if I would clear the rocks from her garden and arrange them in a neat border. Rocks, like icebergs, have a nasty habit of hiding nine-tenths of themselves beneath the surface. What looked like a few hours' work turned out to be a back-breaking, finger-scraping full day, and it was after dark when I gruntingly rolled the last boulder over to one side.

When the woman praised me for the job and asked me what I thought she should pay me, I responded in the spirit of my father's teaching and said that labor in the service of another was itself sufficient reward. That isn't the wording I used but the woman got the idea.

"How nice," she said, "to know someone concerned with spiritual rather than material things. Thank you very much, little boy." And she closed the door.

I didn't have to be hit over the head to realize that there was *something* wrong with that arrangement. In later years when I was negotiating five-figure sums for single appearances, many an agent or producer paid a little extra for those rocks.

However, I had little time for either the past or the future as I rode the rails toward my ultimate destination, New York City. I guess the Art Linkletter drive, the impatience to get ahead that has served me so well throughout my career, first manifested itself atop a boxcar somewhere in the Dakotas where the line crosses from the north to the south state and heads for the Missouri River. For the first time in my life I was really weary. Not just tired, but exhausted to the point where I made a mistake in judgment that nearly cost me my life.

Life was relatively cheap on the road. The distance between living and dying was the few feet between yourself and the knife-edged wheels racing over the track below. Men fell off all the time, killing themselves in the fall, or mangling themselves under the wheels, or severely injuring themselves and then lying for days by the right of way until nature took its course. You got used to it except when you came close yourself. Then it was another matter entirely.

A long—four or five hours—uninterrupted sleep was a luxury that few of us hoboes could afford. What with cars being shunted onto sidings, being loaded and unloaded, or being detached and joined to another train that might take you into cold, freezing weather where it was difficult to survive, it was hazardous to sleep too long. So we slept like cats, always on the alert for any kind of interruption. Even an empty boxcar could be a deathtrap. It was standard procedure on the road to set a stick at the open door of an empty car when you felt that you were going to sleep.

A railroad bull or freightman coming down the line would see the stick and know that someone was inside. A foolish giveaway of the bum's hiding place? Quite the opposite. Very frequently the train crew would close and lock empty cars to keep riders out. Better to be awakened and kicked off than to be locked in on a remote siding until you starved to death.

Refrigerator cars were especially vicious deathtraps. In those days blocks of ice in special compartments at both ends of the car kept the cargo cold. When the car was empty so were the ice compartments, which were reached through small trapdoors in either end of the roof. These compartments made particularly good sleeping accommodations because they were heavily insulated, keeping out the weather and, not so incidentally, the noise. But a bull or a yardman locking that trap on a sleeping bum almost certainly signed his death warrant because the cars were infrequently used and had to make long runs to reach the produce sources where they would take on ice.

Many a time I've been grateful that a trainman heeded my signal—the trapdoor swung fully back so that it lay flat against the roof—and ran me off the train before locking up.

Still, I grew careless in other ways. Like many another young man mastering a trade, I grew cocky as my proficiency as a hobo increased. Rest became so important that I took to stretching out full length on the narrow walkway on top of the freight car and, my body attuned to the gentle rocking rhythm of the rails, I would fall fast asleep. The smallest unusual movement, a sharp bend in the railbed, a sudden stop, the sleeper turning over on his side—any one of these could mean a terrifying roll down the sloping roof and a bone-crushing fall off the side.

I was dreaming this night in South Dakota, flat on my back on the walkway. I don't remember the first part of my dream but I do know that it quickly became a nightmare. Something was threatening me and I was so frightened that I awakened just in time to grasp the walkway edge and stop myself from rolling off. Obviously I had been turning over and that dream saved my life. At the time I simply lay there rigid with fear at my narrow escape. But later I wondered about incidents like that. Had my father's prayers brought me protection, which I was too self-centered to see? *Luck* is the word I used then, but now I wonder, I really wonder.

My success with shows like "People Are Funny" and "House Party" stems partly from a spirit of adventure that dates back to my hobo days. I am always ready to try something new, something different that will move things along. That's why the shows were always interesting and stayed on the air for such a long time. I suppose I owe that let's-make-it-happen trait to my poor father, whose inability to promote anything but his own insolvency made me so much the other way.

I now decided that I was through with freights as I felt a growing impatience to get to New York. I didn't really know *why* I wanted to go there but, like the astronauts and the moon, I had to go. So I broke the news to a dubious Denver Colorado Fox that from now on we were traveling in style on fast, through passenger trains, riding blind baggage.

Riding bling baggage is to a hobo what a triple somersault is to a circus flyer; one doesn't try it unless he is absolutely sure of what he is doing. Well, I wasn't absolutely sure but I was fed up with being shunted back and forth across the country so I studied the habits of the big transcontinental train engineers and waited for my chance.

Every passenger train in those days had a baggage or mail car coupled to the engine tender, the unit behind the engine that carried fuel and water to make steam. Every passenger car had a door at each end that hooked up to its opposite number in the next car and permitted passengers and crew to walk the length of the train. But the baggage car's door facing the tender had no counterpart with which to connect, so it was locked on the inside. A very narrow platform, perhaps two feet wide, jutted outside the locked door. It was there that an adventurous hobo could ride hidden from the engineer and fireman by the broad metal rear wall of the tender.

I remember my first blind-baggage trip vividly. I had to stand up, fully exposed to the wind whipping viciously behind the tender. Directly under me the rail ties streaked by, a ninety-mile-an-hour blur. Nothing was between me and the rails but the metal coupling joining car and tender. With a little experience I was able to dig my fingers into the narrow metal ridge just outside the locked door. Many hoboes died falling off that perch, but for me it was an exhilarating, challenging ride, which finally landed me just outside New York.

As I got my first look at Manhattan, I was ready to take on the world, even though I had only a few dollars in my pocket and some less than fashionable belongings in my canvas sack. But I had a secret weapon that would help take Denver and me through some difficult times.

Chapter Two

Actually I had *three* secret weapons. Two I was aware of and the other I'm just now beginning to appreciate. My two tangible allies were the typewriter and the YMCA. Let me backtrack a little to explain.

This will make a great many dropouts happy and probably disappoint some fans of mine struggling to give their youngsters a broad-based education, but I must confess that the most useful skill I took from high school in San Diego was the ability to type eighty-five words per minute. My story would be better, I suppose, if I could recall a teacher who fired me with a desire for knowledge, or a course that led me toward my ultimate career. But I cannot. Typing was my "major" (I was the school champ) and typing is what kept Denver and me from starving many times in our travels.

You know, come to think of it, I don't feel that defensive about typing. I serve on the boards of a number of colleges and glancing at the curricula I see course credits being handed out for "Urban Communities," "Creative Perception," and, not least, "Oral Communication" (which I can only assume has something to do with talking). So practical, income-producing typing doesn't come off too badly.

Back in my hobo days typing was a much more specialized skill than it is today, so that a sixteen-year-old boy who was both fast and accurate was almost guaranteed a job whenever he hit a city of any size. As for the Y, well, it was my second and, in many ways, my most important home through my developing years. In San Diego I had done everything there from handing out towels in the locker room, to supervising games, to instructing in swimming and basketball. I had a lot of fun just earning my membership privileges but it was the character-forming example of a group of dedicated men called "secretaries" who afforded me a set of basic values I could not have gotten at home. Christians in the broadest sense of the word, YMCA boy's work secretaries gave many youngsters an awareness of day-to-day ethics to live by that stood them in good stead when the going got rough, and I, for one, will never be able to thank them enough.

Whenever I go to the Y college in Springfield, Massachusetts, in connection with my duties as a board member, or to some fund-raising function in another part of the country, I always recall my sense of relief at belonging to the Y whenever Denver and I, usually broke and always tired and hungry, landed at some small-town Y during our more than a year and a half on the road. I would show my membership card and we would always be allowed to sleep somewhere, usually on the padded mats piled along the walls of the gym. And the Y meant someone to talk to, a secretary or a fellowship student working his way up, to reassure us that we had not lost all contact with civilized society and to reaffirm moral values that can be too easily lost while riding the rails. The staffer on desk duty was good for a chit, which got us a wholesome hot meat in the cafeteria. A number of such experiences led me to a less than earth-shattering discovery: the food in all Y cafeterias tastes exactly the same. Whether pushing our trays in San Diego or in Brooklyn, the food, while always plentiful and steaming hot, had a startling sameness. It is not that the meatballs tasted the same in Mason City, Iowa and Columbus, Ohio but that the meatballs in Mason City tasted like the hotdogs in Mason City. It took me a while to figure out why, if I closed my eyes, I had difficulty distinguishing between sausages and hamburgers, or beans and peas. The problem was, to echo a popular television commercial, the water—the swimming-pool water. In those days Y pools were all heavily chlorinated because of heavy use from a wide variety of people (including hoboes) in for a hot shower, a swim, and a meal. The chlorine got into hair, onto skin, into clothes, and, I'm convinced, invaded the palate, where it formed a coating impervious to the culinary efforts of the finest French chef. The food's sameness had nothing to do with the cooks; it was all, one might say, a matter of individual taste.

Occasionally Denver and I would decide that we wanted to spend a couple of days seeing the sights in some town and that meant we needed money. I would put on a clean shirt and reasonably pressed trousers (always kept tightly rolled for an emergency), spit-polish my shoes, and head for the local offices of Underwood, Elliot, Fisher, or Remington Rand. In those days the typewriter manufacturers supplied the machines and both supplied and trained the operators, much as the phone companies do today, and dependable part-time help was always in demand. When I showed up the dialogue never varied.

"Do you need a fast typist?" I would ask.

"How fast?"

"Oh, eighty or ninety words a minute," I'd reply casually.

"Accurate too?"

"Very accurate."

"Ha, ha."

"Do you have a piece of paper I can use?"

Their curiosity always got the better of them, and in no time at all I was out typing inventory, or helping with the billing, or doing some other fill-in job. My earnings, together with whatever Denver garnered, made us respectable citizens, at least until the work gave out or we got itchy feet and decided to move on.

Of course, it wasn't always that simple. We lied a little to stay alive. I remember one time in Minneapolis I was hanging around the employment office and the clerk put up a card listing an opening for an arc welder. I promptly applied and was sent out to the Waters, Genter Toastmaster Company to report to the shop foreman.

"So you're a welder," he said, eyeing me skeptically.

"Well," I said, "to tell you the honest truth it's been some little time since I actually did any welding and I may be a little rusty."

"Where did you work last?"

"It wasn't exactly work," I explained, flashing him my most open-faced, guileless smile. "It was in welding class in high school."

"Some time ago!"

"Yeah," I parried. "I really need this job and I thought you might put me on something else while I polished up on my skills."

Most people are basically decent and the foreman was no exception.

"We'll put you on grinding until you get the hang of welding," he said.

"That's just great," I thanked him. "Grinding's simple enough. I'll be welding in no time."

The only problem was, I didn't know what grinding was either. But the guys in the shop helped me learn the relatively simple job of grinding off the metal bead left after two edges are welded together. I got fired a short time later but not before I had learned something that stood me in good stead throughout my life: never form prejudices based on ignorance. As the Indians say, don't judge a man until you walk in his moccasins.

Those tough steelworkers used snuff. All my reading, both in and out of school, had painted a snuff user as a dandified member of European nobility, dressed in a silk suit and not quite as masculine as he might have been. My face and manner must have reflected my feelings because one of the arc welders, a mountain of a man with a beer-belly and a perpetual beard, put a giant pinch of the stuff up his nostrils, sniffed, and asked me what was on my mind.

I didn't want to get killed so I answered evasively that I thought that only people who wore spats and monocles used snuff.

"You mean sissies?" the welder growled.

"Well, not exactly."

"Take off a shoe and sock," he commanded.

I looked around to see several other leather-faced men watching us; I began to get nervous. I envisioned some kind of inquisitionlike torture involving an acetylene torch.

"Wh—why?" I asked.

"Never mind," my tormentor roared. "Let's see a bare foot."

The others circled menacingly as I removed shoe and sock. I tried to put up a brave front as beer-belly grabbed my ankle and stuffed a big pinch of snuff between my big and second toes.

"Okay," he said. "Put the sock and shoe on and get back to work."

About an hour later I began to get sick to my stomach and shortly after that I began vomiting. I was so nauseated that I had to lie on a wooden workbench as the arc welder and his buddies gathered around. I didn't realize what was wrong until I saw the pleased looks on their faces.

"Would your lordship like his spats removed?" beer-belly asked as the others roared.

I tore my shoe and sock off and stuck my foot in a water barrel we used to cool hot steel. My torturer explained that the nicotine had entered my system through the warm, moist pores between my toes and had the same effect as if I, a nonsmoker, had chewed tobacco or smoked a big cigar. The experience did two things for me: it increased my respect for the constitutions of snuff users and it turned me against using any form of tobacco for the rest of my life. That arc welder did me a favor far beyond teaching me not to judge people too hurriedly.

Back in 1929, on the bum, my thoughts were only of Art Linkletter's survival. Although I realize now that many of my experiences had a deeper significance than I then perceived, I knew only that I was scrambling and was prepared to do almost anything to get by, like pretending to be an arc welder. When finally I got my chance at it, I ruined a whole job, which must have cost the company a few hundred dollars. Today, if someone working for me was that deceptive, he would probably get fired. Which is what happened to me, proving, I suppose, that some of life's realities change very little.

And I deserved to be fired, no question about that. My first and only welding assignment consisted of using an angle iron to join a metal leg to the top of a large thermal table to be used as a steam tray in restaurants. I made the weld and stood back to admire my work as the grinder, a minor functionary well below a professional welder, came over to carry it to the next step. When he reached down and picked it up, the leg bent inward as though on a hinge. My weld had the consistency of chewing gum.

Undaunted, I went over to the stockroom, picked up a fresh angle iron, and walked hurriedly back to try to rectify the situation. Too hurriedly. My path lay between large sheets of Monel metal, the very expensive shiny material used to surface steam tables. One end of the angle iron dug a deep, irreparable scratch along the full twenty-foot length of a Monel sheet, a jagged testimony to my journey back to the work area. I was relieved of my welding goggles and booted out the door.

I wish I could say that my summary departure from Waters,

Genter filled me with remorse and caused me to sin no more, but "doing your own thing" is not a 1970s invention. Denver and I promptly applied for another job for which we were completely unqualified. Worse than that, we didn't even know what the job entailed.

We saw a newspaper ad for busboys needed at the Black Cat, a nightclub located between Minneapolis and St. Paul.

"What's a busboy?" Denver asked.

"Now that's really dumb," his worldly-wise partner answered. "These places have buses that they use to drive people to and from the downtown hotels. They need boys to help the old people off."

"I've never done that," Denver said uncertainly.

"Don't worry," I assured him. "Nothing to it. You just take them by the arm."

That's right. I had never driven a bus either.

The Black Cat owned no buses but did have one of the biggest kitchens I had ever seen, and it containing mountains of dirty dishes. Even back at a Y cafeteria I had never come across a situation like that. But Denver and I were hard workers and by the fourth night on the job we were well on our way to settling down and eventually assuming ownership of the whole place. We liked the way the present owners operated from plush offices that seemed always to be filled with the most glamorous-looking girls we had ever seen.

However, we were gradually learning that few things in life are ever simple. We usually quit around 2:30 A.M. One night after our last shift, around 4:00 A.M. as I recall, someone planted a bomb in the Black Cat and blew up the place. Apparently there was some dispute between rival mobs and it just happened that our mealticket was involved.

Not discouraged, we landed jobs at the Armour meatpacking plant in St. Paul—why we were so determined to hang around the Twin Cities escapes me now—and were assigned to the offal-cooling unit for the princely wage of forty-two and a half cents an hour.

The offal cooler made the kitchen of the Black Cat seem like a garden paradise. We worked in a huge room, about fifty by thirty yards, lined with overhead rails from which were suspended rows of steel hooks. Large metal cans filled with steaming entrails were wheeled in from the killing floor and our job was to hang kidneys, livers, tongues, and other goodies on individual hooks to cool in the thirty-two-degree temperature. Blood ran down our arms and spattered our clothing; it was a terrible job and one which I often recall when someone asks me now about how hard it must be to do so many retakes on a set.

That job in the offal cooler was one of the really low spots in my hobo travels. More than sleeping in boxcars or by the side of a road, more than eating unappetizing food irregularly, more than being wet and cold with everything you owned soaked through, hanging up those entrails brought on a rare mood of depression. And that mood led to another, equally unusual sentiment: returning home.

I have never been a particularly demonstrative person; I've always prided myself on being in control of my feelings, of showing neither excess anger nor affection. But one night in St. Paul, after I had washed the stink off myself and scraped my pants and shirt on a washboard thoughtfully provided by the management in the basement of the boardinghouse where Denver and I stayed, I lay in bed and felt tears come to my eyes as I wondered what would become of me. The memory of that low spot in my life helped condition me, once I had become a successful entertainer, to realize fully the fruits of that success. Most stars let other people handle their business affairs. Not I. I love to make a deal, a fair deal in which both sides do well. I once fired an attorney who came to me after I had signed a contract, and proudly showed me how we had legally, but I felt immorally, bested someone. I always stand up for my rights but I think the fact that I once had nothing makes me bend over backward now to see that the other person gets a fair shake. It's so easy to be tough when you're on top. I think the mark of a civilized man is to put fairness above any temptation to take advantage.

My son Jack, whom I'm sure many of you have seen during his show-business days, now heads Linkletter Enterprises (of which, more later), and with the best intentions in the world, urges me to drive harder bargains than perhaps I would wish in some of our contract negotiations. Jack is leading from strength and I respect his motives, but I also do not forget that Jack never hung hot offal in St. Paul, Minnesota. There's nothing like the memory of a roomful of steaming offal to instill a lasting desire to practice Christian charity to your less fortunate fellow man.

I feel that this willingness to give a little, to see the other fellow's problems and point of view, is one of the reasons I had one show on the air for nineteen and another for nearly twenty-five years. During tough times, when big shows were being canceled all around us, we endured because I was always willing to deliver a little more than the contract called for. And when we were riding really high, number one across the country for years, I didn't come back to our sponsors and say, "Well, you know I'm so hot now that I don't think this is a fair contract." A deal is a deal for me and, although new contracts were naturally subject to negotiation, it was never a pressure thing. I never held success out as a threat to the people who had placed their faith in me in the first place. I cannot help feeling that the current fashion in show business and sports of trying to squeeze every drop out of temporary rises in popularity or box-office appeal will eventually prove counterproductive.

True, one does not become a millionaire by living in fantasyland unless, like the late Walt Disney, he happens to own the place. But I lived a fantasy for the first few formative years of my life because I refused to face the reality of my situation. When I was quite young (I don't recall my exact age, maybe eight or nine) I learned that I had been adopted. I found out about it by snooping in John Linkletter's mail and reading something from the adoption agency that brought my world crashing down. Someone didn't want me. My real mom and dad had gotten rid of me; they had dumped me, it seemed then, onto anyone who would take an unloved, unwanted kid. I didn't know that I had no legal father. I didn't learn about that until my federal indictment many years later, but it wouldn't have mattered, really. I was a castoff, and in the face of that shocking discovery, all the real affection that the Linkletters had shown me was temporarily forgotten.

But human nature is wonderfully resourceful. It was not long until my dismay gave way to elation; I was building a dream world that would sustain me through a very trying period of my life. I convinced myself that my real parents were very rich—maybe even royalty from England—who had deliberately sent me to live with the Linkletters to test my mettle, to see if I was worthy of being the heir to a great fortune. I used to lie at night in my small room and get goosebumps as I thought of the day when a big limousine, maybe even a Packard, would pull up to our front door and my mother, a beautiful woman decked with jewels and furs, would step out to tell me that the testing period was over, that she would take me home.

I would be a little shy with her at first, but gradually, as we drove to the station where my father waited for us in his private railroad car, a warm glow would steal over me and I would reach out to hug her and thank her for not leaving me forever.

I relived those nights in that St. Paul room and came closer to self-doubt than at any other time in my life. Then something inside me, something I couldn't understand, took command. I think in the darkness Dad Linkletter forgave me for my feeling of betrayal, and his prayers, always selfless prayers, pointed the way. The next morning I told Denver that we were hitting the road. New York beckoned, and with it the stock market crash that all but wiped out my first investment and headed Denver and me toward high adventure in South America.

Chapter Three

Our arrival in New York was something less than triumphant. Rail transportation ended for us in New Jersey; our thumbs took us to the Hudson shore where, after due consultation, we decided to dip into our capital and pay the five-cent fare on the 42d Street ferry across the river to Manhattan. New York City is always an imposing sight but to two boys from the metropolis of San Diego, 1929 population approximately 150,000, it looked to be a giant of a place, bigger than we could ever have imagined.

Though impressed, we were anything but cowed. We set up headquarters at the Brooklyn YMCA and then went looking for jobs. I landed my first job on Wall Street! Perhaps it was a homing instinct but Denver and I—as stock clerk and typist respectively—were soon caught up in the heady atmosphere of high finance that made the street a truly exciting place.

It wasn't long before we had rented ourselves more spacious

accommodations—a walk-up double room in an old brownstone on St. Mark's Avenue in Brooklyn. Every morning, along with other aspiring capitalists, I would take the subway to Manhattan and man my typewriter at the National City Bank on Wall Street. I was in the coupon-collection section of the bond department typing in triplicate copies of all the bond transactions, a job with some responsibility that paid reasonably well.

For the first time, I felt the exhilaration of being in the wellspring of major events and I threw myself into the spirit of my surroundings. I was on Wall Street and that meant dressing the part. After a few weeks I bought my first derby hat, some pearl-gray spats, a cane, gloves, and a topcoat—a tipoff, perhaps, to my show-business future. I was, in my own mind, what we might call today a very heavy dude, and on Sundays I would stroll through Central Park letting—I had no doubt—all the prettiest young ladies eat their hearts out.

My projected race up the success ladder to a partnership in J. P. Morgan got me about two rungs off the ground only to be thrown abruptly back to earth by the devastating stock market crash in October 1929. I was right in the middle of one of the truly momentous events in our history, yet I could not fully comprehend what was going on. I was too young and, despite the spats and derby, too unsophisticated to understand the immensity of that terrible tragedy. I know of course that disasters were occurring all around me—suicides in the next block, once powerful men gone from suddenly vacant offices, people gathering in little groups on the street and in restaurants dazed by a world tumbling round them—but my experiences were essentially personal and that is how I recall those troubled times.

I remember, for example, the manager of our typing division; we called him Old Man Hewitt. He was a Scotsman, a man of solid values who had refused to be swept along by the frenzied buying and selling, the recording of paper profits, that led up to the crash. Hewitt was a man you could count on; he was about as frivolous as a Highland peat bog. When during the third month of the crash he gathered us solemnly around him we listened with rapt attention to his pronouncement that *now* was the time to buy common stock. Top management felt that National City stock, selling for nearly four hundred dollars in early 1929, had now bottomed out at around ninety. The bank was showing its goodwill by suggesting that its employees invest before the word got out all over the street.

If Hewitt was for it, I needed no further urging. I knew that, after thirty years of service, this was a big decision for him; he was mortgaging his home and life insurance as well as putting all his life savings into the market. I had saved one hundred and ten dollars and I proudly invested ninety-two of it in one share of National City common, certain that I was building the broad base that would make my future financially secure. Many months later in San Diego, when I badly needed money, I sold that share for eleven dollars. That sobering experience served me well in future years.

One incident during the crash illustrates, I believe, more than any other in my recollection the intensely personal nature of that financial debacle. From a distance we tend to regard the crash as something that happened on an impersonal, institutional level. We know that it caused severe unemployment and hardship, but it seems in retrospect somehow too big, too overwhelming, to be reduced to an ordinary working individual's shattered dreams.

Ironically, the market crisis actually made my job more secure. The spiraling bankruptcy rate resulted in increased traffic in bonds, and that meant more typing of records and reports. So I wasn't hurting and could still afford to eat in one of the small, inexpensive places in the financial district.

One day while eating lunch I noticed a girl sitting by herself at a table by the wall. She had a cup of coffee in front of her and was staring at it, the tears streaming down her cheeks. She was young and pretty and my first thought was that some black-hearted rogue had done her wrong. Her sorrow seemed to possess her whole body.

It may be hard for some people to believe, but in those days I was not all that sure of myself. Perhaps the memory of my embarrassment over Dad Linkletter's tendency to comfort complete strangers restrained me. But the girl looked so helpless and alone that finally I got up the courage to ask her what was wrong. She had lost all her savings in the crash, she explained, and her secretarial job as well.

I remember trying to think of the right words to say, but before I could say more than "I'm sorry" she was gone. I returned to my table aware for the first time that ordinary people like myself, people I saw and touched and talked to every day, were being crushed by the crisis. I've often wondered what happened to that girl and to Mr. Hewitt. How many like them succumbed to the temptation to make dreams come true in the market?

Later on, when I began earning some money in radio, I became a cautious, even conservative, investor, a pattern I held to until I had enough capital to permit me to take a flyer on some product or service without getting hurt too much if it didn't work out. But being conservative can have its drawbacks too. In 1952 the thought of Old Man Hewitt's downfall worked against me; I decided against an investment that would have netted more millions than I care to think about.

It happened this way. Walt Disney and I were very good friends. Walt, contrary to his public image, was a very private person and to this day I'm proud that he and his wife Lillian often chose to spend their leisure time with Lois and myself. In 1952 the Disney Studio was going strong and Walt was doing very well. His studio in Burbank was quite an unusual place. Unlike the other major movie lots, Disney Studio was a family operation and that was the atmosphere that prevailed there. Everyone from grip to producer relaxed on the well-kept lawns and spacious playing fields at lunch time, and most were on a first-name basis. Walt himself frequently joined these noontime gatherings.

Perhaps it was the absence of human stars and the cold, competitive environment the Hollywood system fostered; or perhaps it was the clean family-type product that Walt turned out. But whatever the formula, everyone in Hollywood knew that working at Disney was fun, something that could not be said at the other studios, at least in the same sense. Indeed, to this day Disney loyalty is demonstrated by the studio's second- and third-generation employees, the "Disney families"; not infrequently a "family" member will be moved up the creative scale to make way for, say, a carpenter's daughter to become a script girl or a grip's son an artist in the animation division. If that kind of two-way respect and support be nepotism, then let's have more of it! That's what the American ethic is all about, pride in work and family and, inevitably, pride in the Christian principles that make it possible.

Well Walt, being Walt, was getting restless. One afternoon I'll never forget, he asked me to take a ride with him into the country. We drove for about twenty-five miles through orange groves and fields in a sparsely populated area of Orange County. Anaheim, a pleasant town of middle-class homes and lots of open space, was our destination.

We turned off the main road and drove along some groves until we came to a large expanse of land, uninhabited except for a few grazing horses and some abandoned sheds. We got out and Walt began vividly describing Disneyland: the acres of colorful buildings in places called Tomorrowland, Jungleland, and Fantasyland, the thousands of people parked in huge parking lots, and the thousands more arriving on a smooth, silent overhead monorail from a nearby luxury hotel. Walt could actually see the millions of people coming from all over the world to enjoy themselves in this never-before-conceived magic kingdom.

While he talked, becoming more enthusiastic by the minute,

I began to grow more and more concerned. Who in the world, I mused, is going to drive twenty-five miles to ride a roller coaster? The logistics of the venture staggered me. Walt was proposing to create a city dedicated to relaxation and amusement, with all the financial and construction problems that starting a project like that from scratch implied. He was thinking in Hollywood terms, I told myself. He was building a huge outdoor set that would be for real.

I had such admiration for his business acumen and his show-business savvy that I hardly knew how to tell him that, for once, he was making what would probably be the biggest, most ruinous mistake of his life. Then he came to the reason for asking me there and I knew that I couldn't bring myself to deflate him, at least not right then.

"Art," he said, "financially I can handle only Disneyland itself. It will take everything I have as it is. But the land bordering it, where we're standing now, will in just a couple of years be jammed with hotels and motels and restaurants and convention halls to accommodate the people who will come to spend their entire vacations here at my park.

"I want you," Walt continued, "to have the first chance at this surrounding acreage, because in the next five years it will increase in value several hundred times."

What could I say? I *knew* he was wrong. I knew that he had let a dream get the best of his common sense so I mumbled something about a tight-money situation and promised that I would look into the whole thing a little later on.

"Later will be too late," he cautioned me as we walked back to the car. "You'd better move on it right now."

I well remember that short walk along the dry, sandy road because that little stroll probably cost me about a million dollars a step. But I can look back with some satisfaction to one omission by Walt. He was right about the hotels, motels, restaurants, and convention halls; and right about the millions of people coming there to spend their vacations. But he didn't foresee that they would build a modern 55,000-seat baseball park across the road to house the California Angels. Or did he?

A little side note concerning Disneyland's birth pangs. Walt not only had the capacity to envision the project, but also had the guts to carry it out. And it wasn't easy. Soaring construction costs and unpredictable disasters began to tax his capital severely. Once, for example, an entire shipment of bathroom fixtures arrived too damaged to be used and had to be replaced. True, he had insurance, but by the time the litigation between the manufacturer and the shipper was concluded, Disneyland was in full operation. He had to come up with more cash at the time of the damage. And that happened again and again so that when Disneyland was finally ready for the first press preview, Walt had used all of his assets as collateral to keep his dream alive. And that, to me, represents the essence of America. He has provided jobs for thousands, and pleasure for millions of people at Disneyland. Yes, he has made money. But how many people would stake everything, including their personal assets, on such a gigantic roll of the dice? Remember, Disneyland *could* have been a failure. It's easy from hindsight to say, "How could he have missed?" Well, I thought he was wrong and I've made a few dollars in my time investing in business ventures. I've lost a few too.

Anyway, in 1955, when I first stood in Disneyland during a private preopening tour and beheld the wonders around me, I knew that it would be a success. And I thought of my old boss back at National City in New York whose unhappy example first taught me to employ caution in financial affairs. So many people like him felt that the first bump in 1929 was the big one, that things could not possibly get worse. In reality, the real slide continued into 1932 and took numerous second-guessers with it. On one of my television shows many years later I asked a youngster if he had ever heard of something called the stock market crash of 1929. He thought a moment, then said, "Isn't that when people stopped becoming millionaires and millionaires started becoming people?" In any case, I'm sure that Mr. Hewitt would have understood my reluctance to accept Walt's invitation to buy land. He was a conservative at heart.

In New York, during that cold, damp February of 1930, the crisis atmosphere was beginning to get both Denver and me down. That, plus the weather, decided a couple of California boys to head for warmer climes. So spats in place and derby set at a rakish angle, I applied to the Munson cruise ship division for employment worthy of our talents. My whole manner suggested that even the mention of ordinary seaman duties would be a gross breach of manners by the personnel manager. But since we knew nothing about seamanship, an officer's berth was out of the question. So we signed on as cadets, a category created for young gentlemen taken on as officer trainees for forty dollars a month and keep, a wage not bad for those days.

We were assigned to the S.S. *American Legion*, a stately cargo and passenger vessel of some 18,000 tons plying the New York–Buenos Aires route. We were given second-class quarters on the officers' deck and soon settled into daily routines that involved a lot of hard work.

We were responsible for keeping the white-work, the rails, walls, and roof of the bridge, clean in the face of daily Vesuvius-like soot discharges from the funnels. We manned large brushes and polishers that kept the decks in top shape, and we helped with baggage loading at our ports of call. On our third night out I received what I considered to be my first real cadet assignment involving seamanship: the 12 midnight to 4 A.M. watch in the crow's nest, a station, the third mate on duty in the wheelhouse impressed upon me, of crucial importance to the ship's operation.

I was to watch for lights over the horizon that would be visible to me about ten minutes before they could be glimpsed from the bridge. When I made visual contact, I was to ring a bell, once for starboard, twice for port, and three times for dead ahead. Well, that first climb of over a hundred feet seemed awfully long, but I soon found my seaman's legs and was thoroughly at ease in my high perch. Too much so. My regular cleaning and maintenance duties had continued through the day so that by the time of my first watch (I had a brief coffee break at 2 A.M.) I was ready to relax. The arc described by the crow's nest as it followed the ship's roll, the clear night sky, and, especially as we crossed the equator approaching Recife, the warm, tropical air, lulled me into a sense of well-being. I didn't fight it. I fell asleep.

I got away with it for two watches. The third night I roused myself in time for my 2 A.M. break, glanced over to starboard, and there, less than a mile away, lighted from stem to stern like a horizontal high-rise apartment, was the biggest passenger liner I had ever seen. I pondered my situation. If I rang the bell now, the third mate would *know* that I had been asleep; on the other hand, he would have to be drunk or blind not to see that ship. Nothing to do but climb down on schedule and, as jauntily as possible, report my presence to the bridge.

"Why the hell didn't you ring the bell?" the mate greeted me.

"I did."

"I didn't hear it."

"Well," I leaned forward and spoke confidentially, "I didn't want to get you in trouble."

"What the hell does that mean?" The mate had a limited vocabulary.

"I heard that some of the passengers have been complaining that the bell was waking them up. I knew you'd probably be blamed, but I guess I rang it so softly that you didn't hear it."

I almost got away with it. But he didn't quite buy my story and ordered me up before the captain in the morning. I finished my watch with a heavy heart, figuring that I would be taken off watch and maybe even demoted to below decks, which meant harder, dirtier work and less freedom to roam around.

The next morning—and I can only believe that someone way beyond that crow's nest was looking out for me—a purser had posted a notice that the captain would like to know if anyone on the ship's register could handle a typewriter. I had just finished breakfast and was on my way to the captain's cabin when I glanced at the crew's bulletin board. I stood there looking at it, smiling at my deliverance, then lost no time presenting myself in the captain's quarters.

"You fell asleep on watch," he said.

"Sir?"

"I have a report that you fell asleep on watch."

"Oh," I replied, puzzled. "There must be a misunderstanding."

"You don't know anything about this?"

"No, sir."

"Then what are you doing here?"

"I type eighty-five words a minute, accurately. And," I added hurriedly, "I can write letters on my own." I guessed that the captain was long on seamanship, but ill at ease with the written word.

He looked at me for what seemed like an hour, looked down at the first mate's report on the desk, looked up at me again, then threw the report into his wastebasket.

"I think, Mr. Linkletter, that the ship will be better off with you down here."

A wise and kindly man, with whom I agreed enthusiastically.

Things really looked up after that. After an initial trial period to feel me out, the captain put his complete trust in me, an honor I eagerly accepted because it meant no more deck work or standing watch. He would have a letter to write or something to transmit by radio and would merely tell me the gist of his message, leaving me to compose it in final form. Things were going very well. Here I was, not yet seventeen, having exchanged the precarious lodgement of blind baggage for a far from luxurious yet satisfactory cadet's berth, and now, to boot, was "communications clerk" (my own designation) for the master of a ship carrying eighty passengers and a sizable cargo on a leisurely South American cruise. Not bad.

Although I managed to sever myself from the cadets' more onerous duties, there remained one that I actually looked forward to—Sunday morning seamanship instruction on the flying bridge. Once weekly I joined Denver and three other cadets on the open bridge to learn something of navigation, the mechanics of running a ship, how to steer a compass course, and other arcane naval matters that I found fascinating.

Cadet Linkletter stood on the open deck and imagined himself, captain's stripes on his sleeves, hands clasped behind his back, on the bridge of the *Olympic* or the *Leviathan* and guiding, with terse, incisive commands to the helmsman, that great passenger liner safely around the Horn. Alas, my old nemesis, the third mate, unwittingly cut short my nautical career by reporting in sick for one Sunday instructional period. His temporary replacement, a senior officer with little time for the learning process, made the near fatal assumption that we were seamen who knew what we were doing.

We were coming into port—I forget now which one—and had just taken on the harbor pilot, an excitable little man who paced the deck and began barking orders to the helmsman, me. Even if his commands had been in English I would have been hard put to answer; whatever language the pilot spoke was mixed with enough pidgin English so I could vaguely make out "Port, two degrees" or "Starboard, three degrees." Unwilling to acknowledge my ignorance, I turned the wheel right and left, trying to maintain a judicious balance between the approaching dock and the long forbidding shoreline on either side of it. The pilot's shouted orders now came in a steady stream and he was dancing around as though possessed by a demon.

One does not, I quickly learned, alter the course of a large ship simply by turning the wheel. I had started our bow in a slow, ponderous swing that would have deposited us a hundred feet or so upon dry land, well below the dock. Shouted commands from our officer, the sudden throb of reversing engines, and I was relieved—not only of the helm, but also of any future participation in practical seamanship.

But I was happy with my lot, even though the sprinkling of very attractive young ladies among the eighty passengers were completely unapproachable by Cadet Linkletter. That was one rule I couldn't even bend. Shore leave was in sight, however, and with it I was thrust into female company of a kind that, I'm told, only sailors fully appreciate. I would soon have my first contact with what my father chose to call "fallen women."

Chapter Four

Whores say the darndest things.

But before I go into some of my experiences in the fleshpots of the Brazilian littoral, I'd like you to know Denver Colorado Fox a little better. His friendship helped me out of a tight spot aboard ship.

Denver was one of seven sons of a San Diego plumber. All the brothers were athletically inclined, and it was through our common interest in high school football and basketball that he and I formed a relationship that endured until his recent death. Denver was a wiry freckle-faced kid not given to conversation. He wasn't taciturn; rather, his low-key approach to life projected a stability that nicely complemented my own more exuberant personality.

In many ways we were an ideal team. I was the extrovert, the talker, the instigator; and he was the listener, the sifter, the examiner of options. Back in San Diego it was I who proposed our odyssey. After hearing me out at great length, and no doubt making allowances for some fanciful projections, he quietly agreed to go along, and that agreement sealed a partnership that never wavered through our year and a half on the road.

Once committed, Denver was the loyalest of friends and, despite some doubts from time to time about my tendency to rush toward new challenges, a trusted companion. I can describe him best by saying that if he could read this modest tribute, he would protest that I was making too much of his role in our adventures.

The quartermaster on the S.S. *American Legion* was a 220-pound six-foot-two Dutchman who liked boys. Preferably young ones, about sixteen, on the fair side, and innocent looking. Cadet Linkletter answered that description perfectly, and the Dutchman soon made his wishes known in subtle ways, like trying to get me alone in a cargo hold or watching for a chance to corner me in the head. Strangely enough, I wasn't afraid; although I could never best him in a physical encounter, I nevertheless placed great faith in my agility and quick wits.

And I had Denver on my side. We worked out a contingency plan that kept us within calling distance of each other whenever the big guy seemed to be a threat. We felt that he would be less likely to make an overt move with two of us present, and if he did get rough, we were prepared to take him on.

I really think, looking back, that if the Dutchman had ever cornered me alone, I could have talked him out of his designs, because, when I was a few years younger, I had fended off some adult homosexuals.

A psychologist might say that my willingness to discuss this aspect of my youth shows that I have no doubts about my masculinity. That may be so, but it is not the reason I'm relating these experiences for the first time in these pages. My homosexual contacts demonstrate two things: the importance of a Christian upbringing that gave me a solid sense of right and wrong; and the fact that my natural curiosity, my desire to learn everything I can about people that has led me to a successful career, was part of me even in preadolescence.

Long before the Dutchman did on shipboard, I had been approached sexually by adult men. I first became aware that I might have problems during summer camp. One night the scoutmaster came into my tent after lights-out to tuck me in and kiss me good-night. Now there are a number of ways a young boy might respond to an overture: fear, sexual arousal, innocent acquiescence. In a situation like that, the predator has such a terrible advantage. He not only is bigger and stronger than his intended victim, but is also an authority figure who represents right and wrong. I shied away from this particular fellow, and probably because he didn't want any problems with a reluctant partner, I was not approached again.

The following summer I was out with a different troop and the new scoutmaster invited me on a little nature hike *à deux*. We sat down in a secluded forest area, he broke out a can of peaches (a rare treat at camp in those days) and began telling me about the boy birds and bees. I reacted in an unusual way for someone my age; I became curious about what made the man tick. So, stuffing a peach into my mouth and unaware of his rising libido, I asked him *why* he wanted to make love to little boys.

It was a simple question, posed without guile. After an initial startled reaction, he began discussing his problem with me. Another question elicited another answer and I soon learned that he was living in constant fear because he couldn't control his aberration. He wasn't proud of his needs, he confided, but something in him reacted to a kid like me and he became so aroused that he had to make an overture. If the boy went along, he would take him as a lover, giving him privileges and showering him with gifts for the duration of camp. But if a boy seemed repelled or antagonistic, the scoutmaster would so skillfully pass the whole thing off as a joke that the youth could not be certain that an approach had even taken place.

Now I, he assured me, was something else. He had never come across anyone, boy or man, with whom he could talk about his problem in such an open manner. By the time the last peach had disappeared, he had undergone the equivalent of a therapeutic session, letting it all hang out, figuratively speaking, to a ten-year-old kid who appeared to understand the destructive emotional conflicts that motivated his behavior.

Well, I didn't understand, really, but I *was* curious, and to satisfy my curiosity I had interviewed him. In so doing, he not only had turned aside thoughts of physical contact but was also left grateful for the experience. While in high school I was approached several times, in theaters, at swimming pools, and other public places by soliciting homosexuals. And two or three times I employed the same technique, polishing my questions each time, until I *did* begin to understand (without condoning) the real sickness that causes men to behave like that.

I remember one man who offered to teach me how to drive his car. To a twelve-year-old in those days, driving a car meant a giant step toward adulthood, to say nothing of the prestige involved. I could hear myself saying casually to Denver, "I was out driving Mr. So-and-So's Cord yesterday. Had 'er up to forty-five on the main road. Maybe I can get you in for a ride next time." Now that was really dreaming because none of us in our crowd could imagine being given the opportunity to drive a car.

So I accepted the man's offer and was soon sitting behind the wheel. Then he put one arm around me to show me how to steer while he worked the floor shift against my leg. Once again I wasn't horrified or scared or angry; just curious. Part of the pitch always included an offer to buy me something, so I let my driving instructor stake me to a soda while I interviewed him. I even remember some of my questions.

"Why do you want to kiss me?" I asked. "Why do you want to do that to boys instead of girls? Did your girlfriend do something bad to you? Have you always felt this way about boys? Do you remember when you first started feeling this way?"

My driving instructor told me he was married, with a couple of kids of his own. He confessed he was horrified when he first realized how he felt about young boys. He, like the other men I spoke with, began answering my questions because he wanted to humor me, to keep me happy with a view, I suppose, to a more intimate relationship. But after he talked awhile, he became so engrossed in his own story and problem that he forgot all about his original intentions and we parted on a friendly basis.

How did I know instinctively to employ the interview technique? Why did I face potentially nasty, even dangerous, confrontations without fear and emerge unscathed? I cannot explain it, but I do believe that an all-knowing protective power chose to oversee my extrication and that the beliefs of my boyhood were standing me in good stead.

In later years I have become deeply involved in helping young people, particularly through the YMCA. I never fail to stress, in talks to staff gatherings, that vigilance must be continually exercised when appointing adult males to supervisory positions in boy's work. I draw a distinction between the so-called consenting-adult homosexual who seeks out his own kind and the aberrant within the aberration who preys on innocent children.

The world is changing, and what many of us in show business have known for years has now become public knowledge and gained at least tacit acceptance, namely, that many prominent people in the arts are gay and are no less talented or interesting because of it. Even the word *gay*, now so commonly used, suggests a lightness and an acceptability that the more opprobrious *fag* does not.

As I think back on it, even as a teenager I felt no special animosity toward those whose sexual preferences were different from mine, so long as they didn't try to impose themselves on young people. When Denver and I were riding the rails, we more than once saw a bunch of bums gang up on a homosexual and beat the devil out of him. I felt then and feel now that people who go out of their way to do violence to a gay must be a little uncertain of their own masculinity if they have to prove themselves that way.

A couple of years after our travels, when I was going to college at San Diego State, one of my favorite professors was a tall, blond, good-looking bachelor who taught biology. We became very good friends. Often I was invited up to his apartment to act as a reader—a student who corrects assignment papers—and we had many stimulating conversations. He was one of the sponsors of my fraternity, Tau Delta Chi, which evolved nationally into Alpha Tau Omega. I read for other professors, of geology, psychology, and history—I was almost a straight A student—but the biology professor was a great favorite of many of the students.

Imagine my shock and dismay when he was arrested for homosexual activity with a sailor in a public park. During the long evenings we had spent together there had never been the slightest hint of his problem. What had happened was what happens to so many closet homos when they drink too much. He dropped his guard and went looking for sexual satisfaction with strangers. His career was ruined; he was tried, convicted, and sentenced to a work farm. Yet to this day I recall him as one of the most charming, accomplished men I have ever known.

Not so the big Dutch quartermaster on the S.S. *American Legion*; he had none of those redeeming features. It was thus with a sense of relief that Denver and I joined some straight sailors on shore leave in Bahia, a medium-size Brazilian port north of the Tropic of Capricorn. But it could as easily have been in Rio de Janeiro, Santos, São Paulo, or Buenos Aires—one South American waterfront whorehouse looks like another.

But not the girls. From the beginning I found them fascinating, each different in her own way, each with a personality of her own. I like to think that I really began my career as an interviewer in the parlors of those bagnios. It was my first opportunity to sit in a relaxed atmosphere with plenty of time on my hands and a captive audience more than willing to tell me their life stories. Those girls knew my curiosity was innocent of any desire to exploit or ridicule them; they responded with a warmth that was quite touching.

Two forces joined in an unusual alliance to keep me from getting into trouble during my tours of some of the toughest waterfronts in the world: my fear that perhaps my father was right about what happened to sinners in the next world, and my certain knowledge of what happened to them in *this* one. By the time we docked in Santos, three-quarters of the below-deck crew had venereal disease. Contracting VD is always a serious matter, but back then the cure, when available, was extremely painful. Enough nights spent listening to the anguished howls from the crew's head as they sought to relieve themselves should have rendered the wildest satyr impotent, but such is the nature of the male animal that when next the gangplank rolled out, a stream of eager sailors hit the docks and headed for the nearest bordello.

And along with them, chastened by the evidence of the wages of sin, smartly stepped Cadets Linkletter and Fox. Years younger than the rest of the crew, we captured the fancy of the whores who speculated about our anatomical development and tried to coax us into the bedrooms. I can't really speak for Denver (we weren't *always* that close together), but the fancy ladies' blandishments didn't do much for me. I have always been a practical fellow, given to calculating the odds in any situation, and as soon as the ladies realized that my prime interest in them was sociological, they gave in with good grace and adopted us as mascots.

The standard parlor fare in those days was beer and peanuts. The girls would supply us with both as they sat and talked between tricks. Occasionally—for example, when the ship's stokers all had shore leave at the same time—our visit would become quite protracted and one of the girls would rustle us up something from their own kitchen while we waited. The whores grew quite protective, warning us to stay away from certain bars and restaurants that were criminal hangouts and generally advising us how to avoid trouble. Those whores sure said the darndest things to two young gringos.

The girls tend to blend in my memory, all being young and most quite pretty. Whether I would think them so today is another matter, but there was a certain glamour at the time and one girl in São Paulo typified the members of her calling.

Elena had jet-black hair and big, wide brown eyes that contrasted nicely with her snowlike skin, that white because she seldom sat in the sun. Unlike many of her city-bred North American counterparts, she came from a little village that was no more than a cluster of shacks along a dirt track leading to a paved road somewhere far away. If I recall correctly, the village was actually in Paraguay and the dirt road crossed the border to the paved sophistication of a Brazilian highway. For Elena, as for most of the other girls that young Linkletter interviewed, getting to the pavement was about as far ahead as she could project her future. Most girls in her village were born, raised, and buried within a twenty-five-mile radius. But Elena sensed that there was something about her that set her apart from the others, and that something, her natural beauty, might get her to the highway and to the untold marvels that lay at its end.

Elena was sexy and aggressive; she found her way to the sea at São Paulo. Uneducated, restless, and eager for adventure, she took easily to being a whore, certain, as were all the others, that her occupation was a stepping-stone to bigger things. She really liked me, and when one of the crew told her where I was from and that I planned to return there to attend college, her fascination knew no bounds. The dear little thing was grateful just for the chance to talk with me. Ah, well, she was a good interview.

That Denver and I did plan to go to college was a source of wonder to most of the sailors aboard ship. Unlike today, when computerization has led to small, highly trained crews living in spacious quarters, sailors in those days were just that—career seamen with little formal learning but wide practical knowledge. Almost to a man they encouraged us to continue our education, appearing to take pride in helping us toward that goal. Their reactions to our plans surprised us; we didn't realize that going to college was that big a deal. From then on we were much more conscious of our good fortune and suitably grateful for it.

You know, when I recall those early years and my eagerness to talk with people and the ease with which I established a rapport with almost everyone, I feel a sense of panic that a career for which I was so manifestly suited—eventually communicating with people on a scale beyond even my imagination—became a reality largely by chance. I could have missed it so easily because there was no one to read the signs and guide me in the proper direction.

If this book is to leave one important thought with parents and anyone else charged with the care of young people, it is this: look for the signs in the very young and do everything to help them along a path that they approach only by instinct through some God-given basic talent. The archbishop of Canterbury writes to me about his "call" to serve God in the interests of mankind and that is the way the word is usually used.

Is it any less a call when an eleven-year-old takes a car engine apart and reassembles it perfectly? The prodigies who play Mozart at four or construct a functioning laser at eight are easily identifiable. But how many parents, perhaps because of preoccupation with their own problems, deny a son or a daughter the ofttimes small encouragement needed to translate a taken-for-granted youthful interest into a satisfying, rewarding career?

The signs were certainly there in my case, had there been anyone sensitive enough to read them. Way back in grammar school—I couldn't have been more than ten—I had two great after-school passions. One was basketball. I would spend hours dribbling a ball and tossing it through a metal hoop. Why? Well I liked it, obviously, but, more important, it was a sport that was easily accessible to an itinerant minister's son with no money. That's why black athletes dominate basketball today. Any kid can play it. All one needs is a ball, two hoops, and a flat surface to learn a game that doesn't require a lot of expensive equipment.

I'll not avow that the world was deprived of another Wilt Chamberlain or Jerry West because no one had the sense to scout me. I did play college ball on the first team and taught the game at the Y, but I never did aspire to being a professional.

It was my second after-school passion that should have been encouraged—the kind of encouragement I tried to give my children Jack and Diane, an effort that resulted in great success with one and great promise with the other. Anyway, in San Diego they were building Woodrow Wilson Junior High, which I would eventually attend, near my elementary school. After class, whenever my paper route or other business activity— cleaning yards, mowing lawns, etc.—permitted, I would go over to the unfinished auditorium, mount the stage at one end, and give a speech. Stacks of lumber, sawhorses, coils of wire, and construction debris were my audience as my voice echoed through the cavernous hall. I could, as we say in show business, do ten minutes on a variety of subjects, gesticulating to make my points, pausing for dramatic effect, and, finally, graciously acknowledging a standing ovation.

I liked to talk, to communicate with even imaginary people. What I was doing, without realizing it, was practicing, much the way another youngster might practice the piano or violin. My instrument was my voice and somehow I knew the importance of developing that talent. If someone wanted to play an instrument, or sing, or dance, everyone knew that he or she had to practice. But practice talking to people, to sharpen reflexes geared to audience attention? No one helped a ten-year-old with that crazy notion, so I had to do it on my own.

Later, in high school and college, I specialized in chairing assemblies, leading debating teams, and acting as student liaison to service organizations, such as the Rotary and the Kiwanis clubs. While still in high school I would at their invitation address businessmen's luncheons to tell them how the students felt about the establishment and what we expected from a society we were about to enter, as well as what we wanted to contribute. It was a lot more civilized than offing the pigs or looting a principal's office. And a lot more productive too.

Kids had heroes in those days: Ty Cobb, Babe Ruth, Jack Dempsey, and auto racer Sir Malcolm Campbell, to name a few. My own hero was Elwood T. Bailey, a professional orator in the William Jennings Bryan tradition. Spawned in the Chautauqua circuit, the eloquent and witty Bailey made yearly pilgrimages across the country, stopping along the way to speak, for a fee, on anything from the current political situation to the Elizabethan theater. Chautauqua, a pleasant town in New York State, became in the late 1800s a center for small cultural gatherings that attracted prominent members of the artistic and scientific communities. Around the turn of the century it gave its name to a movement consisting of scores of other "Chautauquas" in widely separated cities and towns. And along this "circuit" traveled authors, politicians, musicians, explorers, and the like, to lecture on their specialties.

The circuit also encouraged a new breed of lecturer, the man who spoke for the sake of speaking and who did it well enough to be paid modest fees. He had to have a strong voice, good diction, an appealing delivery, and be well versed in a great number of subjects. Elwood T. Bailey was such a man.

The first time I saw Bailey orate or perform—*speak* is too limiting a word—I was overwhelmed and inspired. I broke my neck to be introduced to him, and when he saw that he had a real admirer he took time to hold a long conversation with me. He told me about Chautauqua and I, of course, began to interview him in order to learn as much as I could about this Camelot in the East where people did nothing but get up and talk. When Bailey suggested a second meeting the next day, my head really swelled. Despite all the prominent people he had met (I now suspect that their prominence was in my imagination), he found Art Linkletter, debater and fellow speaker, fascinating enough to give him more of his valuable time.

The next day we talked some more, and slowly the conversation got around to my future. No one had ever talked to me about that before and I hung on his every word, picturing wide travel and lucrative speaking offers under his aegis. Well, it turned out that brother Bailey sold insurance to supplement his income and that his concern for my future prompted him to offer me $1,000 in life insurance for the paltry sum of $3.00. So I bought my first policy and to this day I don't regret the transaction. It remains my idea of a fair deal. I got information and advice from him, and he got three dollars from me.

That policy sticks in my memory for another reason—I had to take a physical given by an insurance company doctor. It was my first experience with the detailed questions concerning all the diseases I or my mother or father might have contracted that would have a bearing on the policy. We went through the long list and he examined me and found me to be in excellent health. As he was completing the form I said, hesitantly, "Doctor, I feel I should tell you something; you see, I'm adopted."

He gave the same kind of long, speculative look that I would later get from the captain of the S.S. *American Legion*, then tore up the form. On the fresh questionnaire "Unknown" was written in answer to all questions concerning my genealogy, a situation that persists to this day. Good health throughout my life has not made my being adopted a problem, but it does point up what I think is the only valid reason for a movement now under way to force adoption agencies to disclose natural parents if the adoptees should demand that information.

I think most demands for information are based on emotion and serve little useful purpose; in fact, in many instances disclosure can be quite harmful, breaking a pattern set over the adopted child's formative years and putting him or her in touch with comparative strangers. However, I can see the advantage of agencies being required to supply a medical history of the natural parents, without disclosing their names or locations, in order that the adopted person may be made aware of possible hereditary diseases or conditions such as the Rh blood factor.

But back to Mr. Bailey. I rarely come away from interviewing someone, then or since, without substantially adding to my knowledge of the person or subject. My talks with Elwood T. were no exception. He left me frustrated because, despite his skill and bombast, I detected the undeniable fact that the great days of the Chautauqua circuit were over. I had missed out on a once-in-a-lifetime opportunity simply because I had been born too late. The chance to be heard by thousands of people in a dozen or more states and to make my name and fortune was, I thought, lost to me.

Radio never entered my mind. Nor did it later when, on our return from the Buenos Aires cruise, I suggested to Denver that we strike out for home. If I thought that my return to San Diego meant an end to adventure, I soon realized how wrong I was. I entered San Diego State College and soon became involved in an international gambling operation that took me to Mexico as an undercover agent. There I observed some of the most famous Hollywood stars at play at the height of their fame.

Chapter Five

I lived with Denver's family when we returned to San Diego. The Linkletters had moved to Visalia, a bustling central California town that serves as the supply and processing center for the fertile San Joaquin Valley. I had little desire to live there and they were content to let me try my wings. Now seventeen, I began to make my own way, responsible only to myself and my Christian conscience.

The year and a half on the road had changed me in many ways. I began my journey as an uncertain, curious sixteen-year-old. I grew both physically and emotionally during my travels and returned a solidly built six-footer, a self-confident and reasonably worldly young man ready to test himself and eager for life's adventures.

In large measure I thank my hobo experiences for the self-possession that has served me so well through the years. There is nothing like hitting town after town as a complete stranger

50

and with little or no money, pitting your ingenuity against such circumstances, and then realizing that you can make it on your own merits, no matter what. Walla Walla, New York City, or Buenos Aires—after that trip the unknown held few terrors for me. I was therefore considerably more mature than the other fellows starting college; I had no doubts at all about my ability to survive.

I could not foresee how severely that ability would be tested during my professional life. The average member of an audience does not, I think, fully comprehend the pressures to which a performer can be subjected, because these pressures are faced and overcome completely without the audience's knowledge.

As a viewer or listener at home or in a live situation, you think that you know everything that's going on up there. Well, if the people you are watching are real pros, the chances are you don't. And that's the way it should be. If an amateur spear carrier in a costume epic drops his spear with a resounding clack, he stands flustered, then trips over his own feet trying to retrieve it. But a professional adds a line of dialogue to make the accident appear part of the play. Multiply that situation by one thousand and you get some idea of the unexpected contingencies a star performer must watch for when he faces an audience.

An audience expects everything to go smoothly. The star on view is always to be in command of the situation. After all, he makes several hundred thousand dollars a year as an entertainer. If he looks bad, the audience becomes resentful because the star is, in effect, telling the viewers they do not know the difference between good and bad. Little wonder that performers learn early to be wary.

After more than twenty-five years as a top entertainer, I was tested as sorely as I have ever been in my career. But this will be the first time that anyone knows that a crisis even existed.

Pierre Berton, one of Canada's most outstanding television personalities, had an internationally acclaimed program called "The Great Debate." Aired over the full Canadian Broadcasting

Corporation television network, these debates attracted top talents from the United States and Great Britain, and I was pleased to be asked to participate in a program built around the premise that "Kids Today Have It Too Soft." I would debate against New York author Sam Baker, who would present the negative side. Debating the affirmative, I was expected to agree that a permissive society gives kids too much, too soon, too easily, and that this ends up harming the youngsters because they find themselves unable to deal with life's realities.

Although I never speak from a prepared text, I do have my research staff make extensive notes for a situation like the Canadian appearance, citing sources and statistics to back my arguments. I then spend some time digesting all the data so that they fit into my general presentation.

I went to Toronto, where the program originated, well armed and spoiling for the kind of good, solid intellectual discussion for which the CBC is justly famous. Mr. Baker, Pierre Berton, and I sat in a studio before a couple of hundred specially invited guests to provide the live reaction to our debate. Came air time and Pierre introduced his guests. I was only half-listening, mentally lining up my opening statements. It came as a kind of double take when I heard the moderator conclude with, "Mr. Linkletter will present the *negative* and Mr. Baker the affirmative positions in this debate. First we'll hear from Mr. Baker."

To adjust to the situation took me roughly ten seconds. It didn't matter who was at fault for telling me affirmative and handing Mr. Berton notes indicating I was negative. It didn't matter that I harbored momentary homicidal tendencies toward the unknown culprit. We were on the air, live, and Mr. Baker, surrounded by a mountain of books and notes (obviously *he* knew that he was taking the affirmative), began doing his thing with great eloquence.

The debate format called for the first speaker to give a four-minute opening statement—which Mr. Baker was now enthusiastically doing, making many of what had been my points.

Then I, as the second speaker, would have six minutes. Baker, the original speaker, would have two more for rebuttal, and the debate would be thrown open to general questions and discussion.

I had four minutes to reverse my position completely, without benefit of any background briefing and in the face of someone tossing my own arguments at me for rebuttal. I could very easily have fallen on my face.

But I won the debate.

Here's how I did it. After Mr. Baker had finished his opening argument, my first words were, "I couldn't agree with you more in everything you've said. I too feel that children are too pampered, have the path made too easy for them, and that all this results in a generation ill fitted to survive the challenges of adulthood.

"But," I continued, "I think we need to go further, to probe more deeply into the kids' role in our society because we must learn *why* the younger generation has been given all these things and *why* we have a permissive society. What is the final result of what is happening to us now? We are not being too soft on these kids; we're being too hard on them."

My audience-reaction antennae quivered; I had their interest. Knowing how Canadians feel about skiing, I used that analogy.

"Let's compare life to a grueling, five-mile cross-country race," I suggested. "We are telling our children not to train for that race although other people may be. We are assuring them that they will have warmth and food and, should they stumble, tender care for the full length of that race, even though we know in our hearts that they will soon be out of our sight in places where we can't possibly reach them.

"In our rush to give our children material things, we quite often don't find the time to give them of ourselves and the benefit of our experience. It's so much easier to let the television set or the babysitter keep them occupied while we cater to our own needs.

"All their problem-solving devices are shaped in neat half-hour segments that are not like life at all. The kids become conditioned to getting what they want when they want it. They become calloused regarding violence they see on the tube without understanding how terrible real violence can be."

The audience had little paddles with "yes" and "no" printed on either side. At the end of our opening remarks, they voted with their paddles and we were even. Knowing the circumstances, I was, needless to say, quite elated and went into the open-discussion section of the program with confidence—justified, as it turned out, by an overwhelming final vote in favor of my negative side.

Thinking back to San Diego, I can recall having after my youthful nomadic adventures the same sense of confidence in myself despite the fact that my experience was quite limited. During that first year back, I stayed with Denver in the Fox family's large, rambling home. It was a warm and rewarding atmosphere, a little like living in a hotel where all the other guests have the same last name. From the beginning I had to work to survive, and when I got a job as a house painter's helper I became friendly with Cordy Samuel, my boss's son, and moved in with his family the second year.

If in the afterlife points are given for versatility, my score should take me to the top. I left my painting job to move in with a very wealthy couple named Wilson in the capacity of butler, cook, and scullery maid. But I found the duties too restricting and quit to begin doing a number of part-time jobs, ranging from basketball instructor at the Y to lifeguard to posing for life-art classes. Many an afternoon I stood resplendent in a jockstrap in one of sprawling Balboa Park's more secluded glades while sober young students committed my musculature to paper. Today my semipublic display of near nudity may not seem like a big deal, but it was very daring stuff in those days; I believe that Mother Linkletter would not have approved of her Artie's way of making a buck.

Speaking of being daring, more than thirty years later Lois and I took Diane to see the New York production of *Hair*. You may recall that the show's nudity caused quite a sensation and was deemed very avant-garde. Well, I could tell that Diane was digging it, but that she wasn't too sure about Lois and me.

We returned to the West Coast—it was the year before her death—and she began doing a series of five-minute interview shows for a local radio station. On one occasion her guest was a rock musician named Lee Michaels, and they talked about *Hair*. I recently listened to a tape of that broadcast. Diane commented that she saw *Hair* in New York with us, but that Lois and I—and I quote her now—"couldn't really get behind it. Most people don't really want to see all that on the stage. They don't want to look. It's too heavy for them."

Then Michaels said, "The day of revolution, right?"

And Diane replied, "We're all part of it." Whatever that meant.

As I listened to the broadcast, hearing her voice again, I smiled, and I remembered those naked flower children up there on the New York stage. Back in 1932, I thought to myself, there was a guy standing on a tree stump in Balboa Park who was pretty "heavy" himself. But what can you tell an eighteen-year-old trying to shield her parents from the harsh realities?

Back in college I was scrambling all the time to earn money, keep my grades up, and have some fun too. In my spare time I wrote *The Aztec Follies*, a musical comedy produced at the college. That seemingly innocent diversion got me into a very exciting cloak-and-dagger situation. A student named Johnny Crofton wrote the music for the production and we became good friends. Johnny's two brothers, Ernie and Jim, ran Agua Caliente, a high-class gambling operation just below the Mexican border. Gambling was legal in Mexico, and like a North American Monte Carlo, Agua Caliente attracted the royalty of Hollywood—top producers, directors, and stars like Clara Bow, Jean Harlow, Clark Gable, and Carole Lombard. In the Gold Room, big sums of money changed hands every night. Remember, this was before Las Vegas became what it is today; but even then, rich people traveled from all over the country to gamble and mingle with the stars.

Wherever there are big-time gamblers, there are also small-time crooks trying to beat the house. Jim Crofton, president of Agua Caliente, and his brother Ernie, who was in charge of the gambling, were being ripped off, but couldn't stop the illegal action. The casino was in Mexico, which meant that any new faces imported from the U.S. to ferret out the dishonest players would be instantly recognized; private detectives who might be hired were mostly known to the thieves.

Johnny Crofton, aware of my always precarious financial condition, had asked his brothers if they could give me a weekend job at the casino. I went for an interview to their San Diego headquarters in the delightful old El Cortez Hotel, overlooking the magnificent harbor. After talking to me for a while—to size up my intelligence, appearance, and ability to handle myself, I learned later—Ernie offered me an unusual job. He wanted me to pose as a rich young spendthrift (my first acting role) who didn't mind gambling away his inherited wealth at Agua Caliente. My job would be to watch for hanky-panky between the "outside" men and the dealers and croupiers.

My youthful appearance would render me above suspicion, Ernie reasoned, so that the bad guys would grow careless in my presence. My pay was room and board (no small thing at a plush resort) and fifteen dollars a day clear. I would be supplied with a one-hundred-dollar bankroll with which to play.

I thought fast. It was a very good deal, but this wasn't like applying for the welder's job in St. Paul. If I didn't know what I was doing, below the border, I was liable to end up floating in the Gulf of California. So I admitted that I knew nothing about gambling.

"Forget it, kid," Ernie smiled. "If you *did* know how to gamble, you'd be no good to us. If you were a player, these guys we're after would have seen you around."

Ernie arranged to have his top pit boss, Tony A., come to a specially equipped suite in San Diego to teach me how to play the games and how to spot those who were cheating. From him I learned a few things not in the San Diego State curriculum. It was with rising excitement that I traded my old Dodge for a slightly less vintage California-top Oakland, which, with windows rattling, bore me south to the Hollywood stars' mecca of Agua Caliente.

A real sharpie, I wore my good suit, white dress shirt, and black and white shoes. I concentrated on the blackjack tables because cheating was easier there. I would sit in, play awhile, and watch for a pattern to emerge. The dealer worked with an outside contact, either a man or a woman. Blackjack, or "21," involves both player and dealer. The player begins with a "hole" card face down, then bets on one card at a time dealt face up, trying to come as close to twenty-one points as possible without going over that number. If the player thinks that he's close enough at, say, eighteen, he holds there; the dealer turns up his hole and tries to get nineteen, twenty, or twenty-one. If he does, he wins; if he goes over twenty-one, he loses. But—and here's the important part—if the player has gone over twenty-one *before* the dealer plays, the player loses.

So I would watch for a situation where a player would call for two or three cards, check his hole card, then hold. The dealer would play, come up with nineteen, and offer to pay anyone who had twenty or twenty-one. The player under suspicion would murmur "Twenty," but without exposing his or her hole card. In the quick action of paying off five or six players, the dealer's fast hands would swoop up the cards, pretend to check the hole card, then pay off the player even if the total was over twenty-one.

Eventually I could see a rhythm being established at one table. Players would come and go, but one or two would stay on, winning and losing. Then the pattern would subtly shift as one player began to hit a "lucky" streak. My eyes quickly became trained to count the hands, even though the dealer's fast movements made them a blur of face cards and numbers. So as not to tip my hand, I would report the action to a watching security man; the dealer and his accomplice would promptly be kicked out.

A variation that calls for more skill from the outside partner involved the dealer using a prearranged signal to tell when he was going to break—that is, go over twenty-one and therefore have to pay the players. The accomplice, on cue, would palm a fifty-dollar chip, adding it to his bet pile just as the dealer broke. An honest dealer can spot that quickly, but a dishonest dealer and partner can turn that arrangement into a very lucrative operation.

So every Friday night young college-playboy Linkletter was in the Gold Room, staying through the heavy weekend action and trying to save the house a substantial sum of money in the process. I got to know the professional dealers and croupiers quite well. They would lecture me on odds and caution me not to gamble. I soon found out that, although they didn't play at Agua Caliente, they used their days off to gamble at Tijuana, a border town to the west. When I asked them about it, they would say that they were professionals and knew what they were doing, but that I, an amateur, did not. The real difference, they told me, was that a professional never bucks a losing streak; he'll get out and live to gamble another day. Conversely, the pro has the courage and skill to ride a winning streak and pyramid his profits.

I had a rare opportunity to see wealthy stars and businessmen gamble compulsively—and lose. Occasionally I would read something in the San Diego newspaper about so-and-so going into bankruptcy or selling out to a bigger concern. I would recognize him as a high roller and know the real reason for his financial distress. My experience at Agua Caliente cured me once and for all of any desire to gamble in the generally accepted sense. My idea of risk-taking is speculating in business ventures like oil and gas wells or new products that may or may not make it. I like the thrill of participation, of laying my money on the line; and the fact that it's not the "come" or "pass" line of a casino dice table doesn't make it any less hazardous or, at times, costly.

A favorite ploy of the cheating teams at Caliente involved the arrival of a well-known Hollywood star. In those days I observed the stars from afar; many years later I would tell my friend Clark Gable how he had unwittingly been used by the Caliente crooks.

When someone like Gable came to gamble, the whole tempo seemed to pick up. True, higher rollers than Gable or Harlow played there regularly, but the glamour that surrounded Hollywood is hard to describe to a more jaundiced, television-oriented generation. Suffice it to say that even hardened gamblers looked up from their games to watch Gable walk by. And stars always had an entourage with them—secretaries, business managers, "gofers," friends, and hangers-on. When the star decided to play, these people would usually take over a whole table. It didn't mean that others couldn't play; simply that the personal aura of the star seemed to reach out and surround the table. And that was exactly what the cheats counted on.

If the star was shooting craps, the play of that table was usually overseen by a stickman and two assistant croupiers. I would pretend to be in the star's party and crowd close to the table to watch the action. Sooner or later I'd glimpse someone at one of the ends of the table who obviously didn't belong to the group. Although he would follow the action closely, betting on every roll, he didn't have that "we're having a helluva time" attitude that characterized Hollywood at play.

I would begin to watch the croupier to the right or the left of the stickman, the one nearest the serious player. Although everyone would bet, most eyes were on the star standing directly opposite the slot where the stickman stood at the middle of the table. Soon the pattern would emerge. If the suspect player had bet with the roll and won, he would wave his hand over his chips, ostensibly to attract the croupier's attention but actually to deposit a heavy bet—perhaps a fifty-dollar or a one-hundred-dollar chip—atop his pile. The next day that croupier would be crossing the border into the United States, barred from working any casino in the Baja California area.

My usefulness to the Croftons ended when I turned in an off-duty chef's helper, without knowing who he was, for conspiring with one of the dealers to cheat the house. The chef's helper had a buddy who had a buddy in the front office, and my cover was blown.

I often recall those exciting days as being a perfect illustration of someone being in the wrong place at the right time. Had the year been 1976 and the place Las Vegas, a young college kid adept at spotting crooked gamblers might have found himself with a permanent career. As it was, I had some fun, made a little money, and added another experience to my rapidly lengthening list of encounters with life.

"If you wish to converse with me," said Voltaire, "define your terms." That is good advice when the word *gambling* is being used. In the broadest sense, the United States of America was a gamble. Men of wealth and station, men with a lot to lose, wagered their fortunes and, in many cases, their lives on this country. They were not dissatisfied mobs in Petrograd or Paris with little to lose. Our Founding Fathers were what we now call the establishment (incidentally, most of them had long hair).

Risk is essential to our system. We need people with enough faith in their judgment to gamble their energy, time, and money to achieve some goal. Our country depends on the businessman risking his money, the scientist his years of study and accumulated knowledge, the artist that most inner part of himself, all for the same end: a product, a minor miracle, an idea that will benefit and broaden their fellow men.

But risk is often not appreciated. For example, the protesters of the late sixties thought that somehow, magically, society produced goods, services, and laws that left them free to bray their mostly inarticulate demands. I'm well aware that those demonstrations were often aimed at people like myself, people who had "made it." Well, no one handed "it" to me, and I can only thank God that I was right more times than I was wrong.

And I was wrong many, costly times. What kind of a nut, you may well ask, would risk upwards of five million dollars in the certain belief that if he baked a better pizza, the world would munch a path to his door? Your present master of these ceremonies, that's who. It happened this way.

First of all I must explain that for me, the real kick of being in business involves what I call "stunting," betting on people and ideas; becoming personally responsible for policy decisions and generally following the progress, or lack of it, of whatever enterprise commands my attention. One such enterprise involved pizza-making.

A well-meaning friend of mine told me about a restaurant and bar owner in the Midwest whose liquor license required that he serve food. He wasn't interested in investing in a kitchen and a lot of food-service equipment, so he perfected a technique whereby he would cook a pizza in a toaster.

Think of the possibilities for a moment. All this fellow needed was a refrigerator in which to store the uncooked pizzas and an ordinary two- or four-slot toaster—two items that almost every American housewife has in her kitchen.

No long cooking process, no heating up the oven (this was before microwave ovens), no tedious wait until your pizza began to sizzle. Not only that, but the toaster pizzas were so tasty that the bar began doing capacity business. You could stop in there, pop a pizza in the toaster, have a beer, and be on your way in no time. The sales potential, it seemed to me, was limited only by the number of toasters in America. Pizza for breakfast, lunch, a snack, or dinner would be available without any fuss in just the time it took to toast a slice of bread.

I've never been guilty of thinking small, and this time was no exception. I brought two business associates in with me to invest some money, talked a large milling company into going along with us through a developmental period, and the Toasta Pizza Company was born.

We began a small test program and soon found out why the Midwest bar owner was so popular—his pizzas, custom-made for the occasion, were indeed delicious and toasted just beautifully. We couldn't have been more pleased. But small tests were simply that—tests that cost more than the retail value of the product. Volume was the name of the game, so we built a factory near Minneapolis that could spew out tens of thousands of Toasta Pizzas and introduced them to the public by a multimedia advertising campaign that blanketed the country.

But disquieting things soon began to happen. Proudly I brought the first batch home to Lois and proclaimed Toasta Pizza Day in the Linkletter household. The next thing I knew cries of distress were coming from the kitchen. "The things are gumming up my toaster," Lois exclaimed. "You stick them in, and when they heat up they run all over the place."

I smiled consolingly, assuring her that any revolutionary process was bound to have growing pains. "But not in *my* toaster," she replied, revealing a certain lack of the pioneer spirit that had helped Miss Lois Foerster's family conquer the West—or at least that section of Fifth Street in downtown San Diego occupied by the owner-operated Foerster Pharmacy.

Undaunted, I contacted the factory the next morning to find Toasta Pizza in a state of siege. It appeared that wherever our pizzas were being used, they were gumming up toasters without fear or favor. After much laborious experimenting, we finally had to face the truth: it was impossible to mass-produce pizzas with the quality control necessary to ensure that they would not secrete a gooey substance at the bottom of the toaster when the heat was on.

And the heat was on myself and my partners. In desperation

we tried wrapping the pizzas in tin foil, but the appropriate government agency soon put a stop to that, correctly pointing out that we couldn't guarantee against electrical shock. Then we tried to load the pizza with enough harmless adhesive material to prevent it from running. But we had to use so much that your teeth stuck on the first bite and you practically had to pry your jaw loose with every chew.

I had a deal all set with the federal government to open a second factory in North Dakota, where we would train the Rose-bud Indians to manufacture Toasta Pizza, bringing money into the area, giving the Rosebuds much needed work, and helping the taxpayer. (The federal government has a program whereby it will help train Indians in skilled jobs so that they can eventually become self-sufficient and live as dignified, productive members of the community.) But that fell through.

The entire effort was a total disaster. When the smoke cleared from the burnt pizza drippings, my two partners and myself had taken a bath to the tune of nearly five million dollars. But who hears about that? To the old saw "The rich get richer" might be added "as the risks get riskier."

However, back at San Diego State my thoughts were of im-mediate survival. If I did think about the future, it was in terms of eventually having a few thousand dollars in the bank to ensure my financial security. I entered college with the hope of becom-ing a teacher because that calling seemed to offer me the best chance to communicate and exchange ideas with other people. I had no desire to teach small kids how to write the letter A and count to ten. The rudimentary subjects held no interest for me; I wanted to deal with young adults and teach creative writing and literature, using mostly the discussion method to give the students the freedom to let their talents take them as far as their imaginations allowed.

In truth teaching would be a sort of consolation prize for my lost opportunity of traveling the Chautauqua circuit. I felt, with-out being conscious of the reason for my feeling, that there was a place for me; my true goal was ill defined in my mind because, although I could not know it then, the shadowy niche did not exist. I would create my own Chautauqua on a scale far beyond the dreams of Elwood T. Bailey. In my senior year at San Diego State that guiding hand that had saved me in Walla Walla in a darkened boxcar and had steered me through some potentially perilous encounters reached out once again. This time the all-knowing Master, to whom my father prayed for my safety and success, set me in front of a microphone, giving me a sense of elation and instant fulfillment—a "high" from which I have yet to descend.

Chapter Six

During my senior year at San Diego State I had two preoccupations: a vivacious, petite brunette with a dazzling smile named Lois Foerster, and an announcer's job at local radio station KGB—in that order. I also was captain of the basketball team, president of my fraternity, and did a little studying on the side. I have a very retentive memory and managed to maintain mostly straight A's with minimum effort.

Although Miss Foerster didn't know it then, she had solved my romantic problems: I was going to marry her. KGB ended my search for professional identity and, more immediately, what we call today my cash flow. Heretofore never more than a trickle, the money passing through my hands increased in volume to the beginnings of a rivulet.

Ironically, my wanting to be a teacher led to my start in radio. I served as a "reader" for several different subjects, among them psychology taught by Professor Harry Steinmetz. At one time I thought I might like to teach that subject, so I was pleased to be chosen as an assistant charged with correcting other students' assignment papers. Often Professor Steinmetz would invite a dozen or so of his top students to informal seminars at which some new paper by an important psychologist would be read aloud and discussed.

We began by each taking turns reading, but soon I was delegated to do all the reading and learned something about myself in the process. When we gathered in the professor's office and sat around on chairs, couches, and the floor to hear the paper, I had never seen the material before. Yet I could read it through with little trouble, without stumbling; pausing and giving emphasis at the proper words and phrases, just as though I had rehearsed it for a week. I can take small credit for being able to do that; I am what is called in show business a natural "cold" reader, able to project interest and animation into written matter that I'm seeing for the first time. To this day, it's one of the secrets of my commercial success.

A dramatic script or a piece of commercial copy after a professional actor or announcer is through with it is difficult to read aloud. It looks as though it were written in hieroglyphics, riddled with slashes, dashes, and underlining to indicate pauses and emphasis.

Some announcers have a dozen different code marks, and a few, like myself, have none. When I was on staff at KGB I occasionally would dig out a piece of marked copy that had been read by another announcer on a previous newscast and include it on my own. I would read that item with great difficulty, sounding labored and pedantic, and sometimes stumbling over simple words.

Professor Steinmetz was a friend of Lincoln Dellar, manager of KGB, and recommended me for a part-time announcer's job in my junior year. I don't recall ever being nervous at the microphone. I gave my first station break on the half-hour, "This is KGB, San Diego," and settled back in the announce booth as though I had been there all my life. I stayed on as a nightshift announcer through my senior year.

In 1934 I graduated with a bachelor of arts, and sophomore Lois Foerster decided to transfer to the University of Arizona in Tucson. I am far from the first to observe that the female mind is a complex mechanism. Her decision to leave California at a time when I was doing some of the most intense courting of my life could have been because (a) her parents suggested a cooling-off period, (b) she wanted time to think things over, (c) I hadn't made that big of an impression, or (d) she just felt like doing it. Or it may have been that I unwisely compared my worldly attitudes with her narrow San Diego-oriented convictions. In any case, I couldn't understand how she could tear herself from a real charmer like me, who overnight had become a celebrity. After all, I was a radio announcer. Not only that, I did remotes!

In those days remote broadcasts had a glamour all their own. Later they became something of a burden, usually assigned to the newest member of the staff, but back in the thirties a remote announcer was show biz transported to your local Kiwanis luncheon or ballroom. I took Lois on my first remote, announcing for the Freddy Martin band from the Mission Beach Ballroom. I got her a place beside the bandstand, took the engineer's cue, and at a standup mike right in front of the band with the whole crowd looking on in awed silence, I said: "From the Mission Beach Ballroom, the music of Freddy Martin and His Orchestra, with songs by Eddie Stone and the Martin Men."

The band hit its theme, I beamed at the crowd, winked at Lois, and went through the elaborate ritual of turning the page of my script, projecting the serious matter of introducing the first number. Heavy!

Three weeks later Lois left for Arizona. Some girls just don't know a good thing when they see it. Anyhow, the bottom line was that we corresponded regularly, visited whenever possible, and she returned to San Diego after one year.

That was some year for me because it marked my total commitment to radio and to every other aspect of entertainment that involved using my voice. I began to take the concept of remote broadcasting and remake it in my own image. Without being aware of the far-reaching implications of my actions, I was pioneering a new type of radio broadcast, one that would be taken as a matter-of-course by millions of listeners in the years to come. But at the time it was so innovative that, a couple of years later in San Francisco, it very nearly did me in.

In 1935 a remote broadcast involved a studio engineer taking a control panel, microphone, amplifier, and some other technical equipment to the designated location and "patching in" to a leased telephone line. The setup didn't provide studio-broadcast quality, but compensated by conveying the excitement of being *live*, whether the scene of action be a big dance band, a ship docking, or a speech by the mayor. These days we take so much for granted that it's hard to conceive that these broadcasts were all from fixed, prearranged places. Not until the advent of wire and tape recorders could radio cover spontaneous events like fires or riots; but even then, such coverage wasn't live: there was a time gap while the recording was rushed back to the studio and played as a delayed broadcast. Now, of course, mobile transmitters, microwave relays, and satellites bring us special events from anywhere in the world as they occur, often affording us a better view of the action than those actually at the scene.

In the mid-1930s the remotes were far from spontaneous. One didn't hook up all that equipment without knowing pretty much what was going to happen, although more than once the best laid plans of network executives went astray in situations that challenged me professionally.

For example, I had been hired as the radio and communications director of the great 1935 San Diego Exposition by a loping, jug-eared public-relations genius named Clyde Vandeburg, beginning a personal and business relationship that continues to this day. Clyde wanted the nation to know that on May 29, the greatest world's fair ever to be promoted by a city the size of San Diego would open its gates. To make sure that no one missed the message, he enlisted the aid of the United States Navy's Pacific Fleet. Like all great promotions, Van's idea—if somewhat ambitious—was simple: he would have the fleet steam into San Diego harbor with the event broadcast live coast-to-coast on the CBS Radio Network while yours truly described the arrival that was to coincide with the fair opening.

As you may imagine, the publicity coup required a great deal of preparation and coordination. All was in readiness as air time approached and the fleet was reported steaming dutifully toward the great harbor where Art Linkletter, surrounded by navy brass, the mayor of San Diego, and any other notables that we could muster for the occasion, stood at the dockside microphone.

But an hour before air time a massive fog bank started rolling in toward the harbor entrance. By the time I got the cue that we were live network, I couldn't even see the dock edge in front of me, let alone the Pacific Fleet now prudently riding at anchor some miles from the impenetrable white curtain.

Without hesitation, I began bringing the fleet in.

The coast-to-coast audience listened with rapt attention. I described the destroyers knifing their way through the harbor entrance, followed by the light and heavy cruisers; and, finally, the stately battleships heaving into view, capping the mightiest display of naval power this reporter had ever seen. The San Diego Exposition was emblazoned on the minds of millions of listeners, who we fondly hoped would now make plans to visit an attraction that had drawn the power of the Pacific Fleet to its very doorstep.

Nationally we were a smash, but locally we created a minor crisis. Residents in homes overlooking San Diego harbor sat by their radios listening to the fleet come in and looking out at a massive fog bank.

As my description grew more animated, taking in such details as the admiral's flag and the rows of sailors lining the decks, local listeners began doubting their sanity. By the time we went off the air, the fleet was still safely offshore, the harbor was still enclosed with fog, and I was feeling very pleased with myself despite some irate calls from people who didn't appreciate the demands of network radio.

The exposition was a smashing success and led to another phase of my rapidly expanding career. But first I had to learn the basics of being a staff announcer in a relatively small station that was part of the CBS Radio Network. So I gave station breaks, read commercials, creating my own background sound effects, did newscasts, and played records. We didn't call ourselves disc jockeys in those days; we merely played those old 78-rpm records that lasted about two minutes and forty-five seconds, gave the weather, read a public-service announcement or a commercial in between, while preparing our next newscast by running out to the newsroom to clip the local newspaper or tear a sheet off the news-service wire.

It wasn't many weeks before Lois was, I hoped, being suitably thrilled at hearing our personal favorites sung by Donald Novis or played by André Kostelanetz over the airwaves. More than one young announcer has learned the rewards of being able to have his girl tell her friends, "He's playing that just for *me!*" I never thought of Kostelanetz as anything but a somewhat mystical figure who conducted magnificent orchestras that played wonderful music. If someone had told me that we would become friends—not long before he died I dined with this dear, charming man—I would have accused my seer of being off his rocker. I have never lost my sense of reverence for the conductor's outstanding talent. Those of us who dream often cannot project those dreams as far as reality will take us. Lois, for example, as chairwoman of the Achievement Rewards for College Scientists, now regularly hires Freddy Martin and his band to play at fund raisers for scholarships to send outstanding science students to a university. It's a strange world, governed, it would seem, by an all-seeing guiding hand.

In the thirties every duty announcer had a favorite program that usually lasted for a half-hour and was played on large, wide discs called ETCs—electrical transcriptions. Programs like "Tarzan," "The Shadow," and "Suspense" came to the studio on two of these discs. They were usually recorded only on one fifteen-minute side, and the announcer would "segue"—that is, switch power from one turntable to a second so that the half-hour program was played uninterruptedly. All one had to do during one of those drama shows was to be there for the fifteen-minute changeover. Consequently, we announcers favored the ETC, *any* ETC. And the more the merrier, because they gave us free time to read, study, or court the young ladies who invariably hung around the studio watching through soundproof glass as the magic figures inside talked into a microphone and, wonder of wonders, sometimes went out to talk to them.

I did my share of studying during my senior college year, but I also broadened my education in other, more entertaining and practical ways. Station KGB was located on the roof of the Greyhound garage, an extension of the Pickwick Hotel on Broadway in downtown San Diego. The Pickwick was a favorite of the sailors from the naval base and did capacity business whenever the fleet was in.

The Greyhound garage jutted out from the hotel in a ninety-degree L, and the sailors, unaccustomed to having blinds over their portholes at sea, seldom bothered to pull down the windowshades while entertaining through the evening. From the announce booth I had an unimpaired view of six floors, and soon developed an expert's appreciation for the innovative and imaginative use of the sailors' particular art form. As the weeks wore on I grew selective in my viewing but never jaundiced. More than once, while I was held enthralled by some rare gymnastic display, the first half of an ETC program would run out, leaving nothing but dead air, or a 78 recording would end with the needle stuck in the last groove repeating the final notes.

The best window-watching time began around eleven o'clock, when we had a popular music program featuring some of the top recorded bands and vocalists. But if I saw something especially good going on at the Pickwick, the radio audience would suddenly hear a selection by the Boston Pops sandwiched between Ted Weems and Skinnay Ennis, because the larger red-label classical selection ran fourteen minutes, giving me more time to study the finer points of the live performance.

After I gained experience, another announcer was hired to do the studio work and take over the Pickwick-viewing duties and I was sent out to do more remotes. I soon discovered that for the most part radio was a formalized, stilted medium, bound by rules that no one had really made up but that had simply evolved. Radio was so young that there were no experts; everyone was improvising as new problems arose.

The very appearance of a microphone at a mayor's press conference or a dinner honoring a visiting politician frightened people. Men accustomed to speaking before large crowds became tongue-tied when confronted by a microphone. Prominent citizens wouldn't dream of speaking over radio without a carefully prepared script, and only the rare public figure would engage in an extemporaneous question-and-answer session without first knowing all the questions and carefully memorizing the answers.

I was sent out to cover only important occasions, or occasions attended by celebrities whom, presumably, the listeners would be thrilled to hear on their home sets. One day I was down on the liberty dock where officers and men from newly arrived ships came ashore in small tenders when I did something spontaneous that changed my whole life.

I was to interview an admiral who had been involved in some newsworthy action, but his launch from the ship was delayed. Came air time and I was on live, looking out at the fleet anchored in the harbor (being able to see the ships was no help this time)

and surrounded by the wives, children, and sweethearts of sailors soon to come ashore. I turned to a sailor's young wife standing
a respectful distance from the radio equipment and motioned
her over. I found out her name and asked her how she felt,
about to see her husband for the first time after six months at
sea.

Before I realized it, the admiral was forgotten. I talked to first
one and then another of the waiting group. I guess it's no news
to anyone that I can put people at ease in front of a microphone
or camera, but back then *I* didn't know I could. So there was
a wonderful discovery on that San Diego dock. I enjoyed finding
out about the crowd, and, once the first strangeness had worn
off, they reacted well to me, as though I were an old friend
sitting in their living room.

Toward the end of our air time, the admiral arrived. I asked
him a couple of questions, he answered as though the whole
thing were a damned-fool way of spending his time, and I signed
off.

Driving back to the station I had mixed emotions, to say the
least. I knew that I had done something unusual for radio at that
time and I felt good about it. But I also was well aware that the
admiral had been on for only approximately ninety seconds, and
the whole purpose of the broadcast had been to publicize fleet
activities.

Listeners didn't phone radio stations the way they do today;
the idea of actually talking to one of those disembodied voices
was rather startling. But the listeners did *write*, so it wasn't until
a couple of days later that I was completely vindicated. The mail
ran heavily for me, as the saying goes, and the "art" of conver-
sational interviewing achieved an auspicious beginning.

I quickly learned something else: not everyone could do the
informal man-on-the-street interview. Even today, truly accomplished interviewers are rare. Because of the very nature of the
profession, an entertainer possesses a substantial ego; but as an
interviewer, he must subordinate that ego and make the *other*

person the center of attention. The audience should be interested in what the person interviewed is saying, what his opinions are, what makes him tick. But an interviewer must have a rare knack to bring out all that, to let everything bounce off himself, and not to intrude his perhaps more forceful personality into the proceedings. The next time you tune in on a talkshow, concentrate on what the guest and host are saying, whose opinions you are really hearing. You may be quite surprised. Merv Griffin interviews, William F. Buckley *debates*; there is a difference.

That's why my shows had such a long track record. Few of the public knew what I was doing, they knew only that they liked it. I'm a catalyst who encourages people to be themselves. In any form of art or entertainment—whether it be a painting, book, movie, stage show, or "natural fun" television or radio program—if the viewer is not aware of the technique employed, then the result is more likely to be a complete success.

In San Diego I was exploring—timidly at first, then with increasing confidence—the possibilities (nearly limitless, as it turned out) of making the general public an integral part of whatever entertainment was offered.

For example, I began unscrewing the heavy "Sure" microphone, the one that looks like the barred front of a midget jail cell, from its stand and carried it around into whatever audience I faced. As a technological breakthrough, that scarcely ranks with the invention of the radio tube or the transistor, but it nevertheless had a profound effect on radio programming as it exists to this day.

My new mobility dramatically changed the relationship between performer and audience. The public had been conditioned to view 1930s movie stars from afar, as untouchable objects that the average person would never dream of meeting. Emerging radio personalities were in much the same category with the added mystique that they were disembodied voices, scarcely real people at all.

Well, I was no big cheese nationally in 1935 but I was coming on pretty strong in San Diego, so when Art Linkletter of KGB stepped off the stage, sat in a vacant seat, and, microphone in hand, began laughing it up with the folks, the result was the humanizing of radio programming. I really wanted to know how you, a mechanic, an accountant, or a housewife, felt about the issues of the day; and your opinions were actually heard by cousin Minnie as far away as La Jolla or Encinitas, a few miles up the coast.

Today the minicam, the television camera that you see being carried on the shoulder of a technician at sporting events or political rallies, is accomplishing somewhat the same thing visually as the roving microphone did aurally. The minicam has its own built-in transmitter that frees the camera to transmit pictures from almost any perspective. Television all seems so smooth now, so self-assured, but when it began to have a national impact, it too was groping, the way radio was in the 1930s.

When "People Are Funny" was a top-rated radio network show in the country it was deemed a natural for television. I recall attending a board meeting of six-figure broadcasting executives in New York to discuss that possibility. It was their solemn belief that all television would originate from New York and all programs would be in twenty-minute segments because no one could be expected to look at that little screen for longer than that. Remember when TV dramatic shows *were* twenty minutes long?

So much for the instant experts. In San Diego I was taking the radio medium past the stage proscenium both literally and figuratively and giving a whole new dimension to the art of conversation. Two friends exchanging news and views could now · share their sorrows and laughter with hundreds of thousands of people who reacted with interest and understanding because similar things were happening in their daily lives. For the first time the public could relate directly to what was coming from their radios.

I remember sitting in the announce booth at KGB during a

slow night at the Pickwick listening to a feed we were taking from a CBS station in Texas. The show, "Vox Pop," consisted of a series of interviews with passersby conducted by two performers named Butterworth and Johnson who asked the public their opinions on the news events of the day. A great white light dawned over young Linkletter's head as I saw the possibilities of that kind of program. I felt that I didn't have the background, temperament, or training to be an actor and I had no intention of reading commercials and news for the rest of my life, but I knew that I had a place in radio. That evening, listening to "Vox Pop," I became absolutely certain of what that place would consist, although I had no idea how far it would take me. *Revelation* might be too strong a word, but something or Someone reached out to give me a direction in life.

The progression from my first man-in-the-street interviews, to simple quiz shows involving little more than spelling words or supplying the last names of movie stars, to the pyramiding prizes of the national quiz shows is history. John Guedel, Ralph Edwards, and I pioneered the true audience-participation show. We used elaborate stunts extending through days and weeks that were not without incidents both humorous and hazardous. I think you might enjoy reading about some of them.

First I must reveal a phase of my career that will give you an idea of the behind-the-scenes battles constantly fought among many celebrities. Even in these days of instant confession there are pressures on stars the average viewer or listener cannot know about. Incidentally, this craze to rush into print with one's latest indiscretion—if Mr. Big Star is caught *in flagrante delicto* with his boyfriend, he immediately writes a book about it—has accounted for the decline and fall of the powerful gossip columnist, who at one time could dictate her own terms to star and studio because she knew so much about the often lurid private lives of the Hollywood elite. It's hard to imagine in this full-disclosure atmosphere what revelation could possibly shock enough to give any columnist comparable powers today.

Let me jump ahead for a moment. I moved on in radio from San Diego to San Francisco, to Hollywood, back to San Francisco, then finally to Hollywood to stay as the originator, along with my partner John Guebel, of two highly successful shows, "People Are Funny" and "House Party." I began, for the first time, to make good money and I moved into Holmby Hills on Mapleton Drive, a street populated by many of the who's who in Hollywood.

It seemed to the national audience that I had it made. A personable, unflappable host heard by millions every week, living in a Hollywood glamourland, hobnobbing with some of the most famous names in the world. The reality was much different. No one watching my shows or listening to me could possibly have realized that I was going through a very difficult personal experience. The majority of Hollywood's upper crust treated me at best as a second-class citizen to be viewed with suspicion and hostility, and deliberately excluded me from their select inner circle.

Why this came about and how a baby elephant helped me out of a most unpleasant situation reads like a movie script, except that in my case it's true.

Chapter Seven

P eople Are Funny" was not the kind of show that I would have listened to or watched. Art Linkletter the listener or viewer would have tuned out Art Linkletter the entertainer, especially during the program's early years.

When we were riding high with "People Are Funny" and "House Party" I would enthusiastically endorse quality programming on the other networks. Put Edward R. Murrow or "Dupont Show of the Week" or "Studio One"—the programs that appealed to me personally—opposite me and I was overjoyed because I knew that I would kill each one, that my ratings would soar in direct ratio to the high-mindedness, the significance, or the profoundness of the shows on the other stations.

Conversely, I looked uneasily over my ratings shoulder when Milton Berle, Eddie Cantor, or Jackie Gleason moved into my time slot on a rival network because I knew that they would draw from my audience. Although I took pride in making "People Are Funny" the best in its class of program, throughout those years of network success I was painfully aware that it was a very lightweight operation.

Our show was almost embarrassingly slapstick entertainment—squirting water on people or getting them to fall into swimming pools with their clothes on, etc. The pratfall type of comedy did have its funny side, but the reason I particularly liked "House Party" was that its half-hour five-day-week format gave me the opportunity to develop a confrontation that elicited humor from my participants rather than make them the brunt of the joke, as so often happened in "People Are Funny."

The difference in the humor is basic. On "House Party" I would talk to you and bring out the fact that you had been letting your boss beat you at golf over a period of months as part of your campaign to get a raise. All the while, without your knowledge, your boss would be sitting a few feet away listening; and at the appropriate moment, I would bring you together. Now that's funny, because the laugh arises out of a real situation. That humor is quite different from my telling you that you have five seconds to remember your social-security number, and if you can't come up with it, you get hit in the face with a pie.

The pie-in-the-face number was never as interesting to me as the interviewing skill required to get selected audience members to say what I wanted them to say without their realizing that they were being set up. The basic difference between what we did and what is currently being done on the game shows involves the producers' and the emcees' attitudes toward the participants.

You may recall the quiz-show scandals of some fifteen years ago, when it was revealed that contestants vying for hefty prizes had been given the answers and were, in fact, behaving hypocritically as they pretended to strain for the correct solutions. It's now illegal to give out answers in advance, but I think that contestants are being told something else that is equally iniquitous: namely, how to act. I mean *exactly* how to act in any given situation.

The attention span of the average television viewer seems to lessen every year. Programs, especially the tremendously competitive quiz and game shows, must be fast-paced with every minute of air time filled with excitement and suspense, no matter how inane. People are chosen from the audience for their scream quotient, their ability to react hysterically to the slightest stimulus. Production assistants jump up and down, wave their arms, and mimic howls of glee just off camera so that the contestant, perhaps awed by the lights and cameras, will not forget how to act at the proper time.

On "House Party" I took time with the contestants on camera to get them talking about themselves so that the upcoming gag had some relevance to them as persons. We did not create instant enthusiasm or surprise; we built to the peaks naturally so that our participants became personalities in their own right rather than robots reacting in a programmed manner.

Here's a perfect example. Have you ever thought how you would really react if someone announced that you had just won $25,000? Well, I know how you would because for more than twenty-five years I had the pleasure of telling many a lucky individual that he or she had won large prizes, like completely furnished new homes, and with few exceptions the initial reaction was a hushed "I won it . . . I won it," or, after a long pause, "Wow, I can't believe it." The initial shock stuns and awes rather than excites. After the shock had worn off we had smiles, hugs, and warm feeling to enthusiastic audience applause. A human being, someone with whom the audience identified, had some good fortune and everyone felt happy.

Today, before a show goes on the air the warm-up announcer asks something like, "Who's here from Topeka?" and a housewife who has been watching the show for months and has made the trip hoping to get on, jumps up on her seat, waves her arms over her head, and shouts, "Me, me, hah, hah, hah." And so it goes. The home viewer catches on fast and knows how to behave if he expects to get on the air. The production people make their selections, and Mrs. Topeka and the others are told to watch the "Applause," and "Louder" signs and to follow the directions of the monkeylike characters with the portable headsets who will direct their behavior. The result is that every show is instant hysteria, with little time given to the individuals as people.

The modern contestant is coached closely as to when to be agonized or exhilarated, when to scream in surprise, or when to giggle excitedly. He or she is cajoled to cooperate, even threatened with expulsion if the show pattern is not followed. The result is caricature.

"House Party" presented people as human beings. Today we see only participants behaving in a predictable, phony fashion that does little credit to the television industry.

A whole segment of this business has for me become totally artificial and unbelievable because the level of reaction is getting higher and higher, to the point where there is no contrast, nothing to relate to, and the drama of building to the sudden surprise is lost. The reason we had such consistent success is that I was and am truly interested in people and that interest communicated itself to millions of listeners across the country.

However, my situation on Mapleton Drive, where I lived for the first time as an established public figure, was somewhat different. My neighbors were, for the most part, motion-picture stars accustomed in their daily work to read a line or repeat a scene twenty, thirty, even forty times until the director got the right take on film. I was surrounded by the royalty of Hollywood, who would no more dream of mingling with their fans or performing ad-lib than driving last year's Cadillac. There were certain things a star didn't do, and this character named Linkletter, who had the nerve to move onto "their" street, was becoming as well known as—and even better known than—some of them. Clearly, the neighborhood was going to hell.

Lois has always been a very private person and I enjoy the company of close friends, but when you're on your way up and have achieved a certain prominence you like to be accepted by your peers, in this case celebrities whose names, like my own, had become household words. Nothing doing. And it wasn't long before I realized why. My whole *shtick*, an easygoing familiarity with audiences that produced entertainment in a relatively unpredictable atmosphere where I might be called on to get out of tight situations extemporaneously, was a threat to the movie personalities. I represented a breach in those carefully built-up and guarded studio walls through whose gates only the anointed passed.

Clearly Linkletter was to be kept at arm's length so that when he finally fell on his face his descent wouldn't tarnish the Hollywood establishment. Well, I'm human and, with a growing family and an attractive wife, I wanted acceptance. I felt that if my neighbors would just come down from their pedestals long enough to meet us, everything would be fine. That finally happened, because Lois and I went on a trip to India.

Prime Minister Nehru had a nickname, *Chatah*, meaning "uncle," because of his great rapport with children. He liked nothing better than to be in the company of youngsters and, through the U.S. State Department, knew of my own relationship with kids. It was our pleasure and honor to be invited to meet him and to hear him address Parliament in New Delhi where we very nearly got thrown out. We were sitting in the diplomatic gallery directly overlooking the speaker's podium and Lois crossed her legs. An attendant came hurrying over and motioned for her to uncross. She did, but a few minutes later, engrossed with the prime minister's speech, she absentmindedly crossed them again. The attendant was on us in a flash with a sterner warning. Duly chastened, she kept her knees primly together for the remainder of the session.

I yield to no man in my appreciation of Lois's legs, but I really didn't feel that they could turn on the entire Indian upper and lower house so I made discreet enquiries. It seemed that with legs crossed Lois was unwittingly aiming the leather sole of one shoe directly at the prime minister's head, a gross insult, according to Indian custom.

We had a nice visit with Nehru and he offered us the hospitality of his country, assigning us a marvelous little woman named Kamela Devi Chadapaya as our official escort. She was head of the cottage industries, an important position because much of India's light industry was dispersed through thousands of small villages whose inhabitants produced textiles in their homes. It was our guide's job to coordinate this vast interlocking network so that the factories in the large, urban areas would have a constant supply of the right goods with which to make the finished products.

When she learned that we planned to go to the great city of Bangalore, Mrs. Chadapaya arranged for the governor of the state of Mysore to greet us officially in what we thought would be a small, informal ceremony. Imagine our surprise when we were met on the steps of the governor's mansion by a full military band. After courtesies had been exchanged we stood and watched four baby elephants, all decorated with flowers, paraded solemnly in front of the steps. It took me a few seconds to realize that I was expected to choose one of the delightful little animals as a gift from the children of Mysore to the children of the United States.

The turbaned keeper in charge of the elephants took me aside and pointed out that although there were three males and one female, I should take the female because after forty years the males go through musk, which I suppose is the equivalent of the female elephant menopause, and become quite ornery. So I carefully weighed his advice, just as though I expected to have an elephant around the house for that long, and dutifully picked the female.

There was nothing we could do but agree to have her shipped home, with an accompanying elephant "boy"—a friendly, aging toothless fellow who looked nothing like Sabu—to our Mapleton Drive address. At the time I was on the board of directors of the Flying Tiger airline, so I had our elephant flown from Bombay to London where Flying Tiger picked it up and flew it to Los Angeles via New York.

We got a little mileage out of its arrival in Los Angeles. I had the mayor there to accept it officially, and then, with due ceremony, we put the elephant and her keeper aboard a truck and soon had them safely ensconced in our garage in Holmby Hills. Our children, of course, were overjoyed and I soon noticed an interesting phenomenon taking place.

Here we had been living next to stars like Humphrey Bogart, Lana Turner, Judy Garland, and Alan Ladd, and composers Sammy Cahn and Hoagy Carmichael without very much direct contact between their children and the "radio kids." Suddenly that began to change. Everyone on the block owned a Rolls Royce and had a swimming pool and tennis court, but not everyone had an elephant in his garage. No one could match our status symbol and our garage soon became the neighborhood hangout. Sammy Cahn got up a mock petition signed by some of the others, pointing out that the area wasn't zoned for elephants and that living downwind of one was anything but pleasant.

Which led me to observe a second interesting phenomenon. By some quirk of nature that little animal could take in thirty-five to forty pounds of hay per day and produce what seemed like sixty to seventy pounds of steaming residue. We simply couldn't keep up, so, after several "elephant parties" that broke the ice once and for all, we gave her to the Los Angeles Zoo and sent the elephant boy back home.

That being the son or daughter of Art Linkletter carried burdens as well as the more obvious joys became starkly apparent at the time of Diane's death. We were and are a loving family, brought up with a strong Christian sense of right and wrong. However, when the children had to go out into the world and

exist away from the family structure, love and a sense of belonging were often put severely to the test.

I knew all this as our family and my fame grew, but I don't
think I fully realized the problems involved, what my children
had to face because they bore my name, until they were all older
and more able to discuss it with me as adults. I think the best
way to tell you this most important facet of my family's experience is to let Sharon, since Diane's death our youngest, now
a mature woman living her own life, recall some of her early
difficulties. I've asked her to write them down. Some of her
observations are being seen by her dad for the first time; I
present them unedited, but reserve the right to comment.

"Well, Daddy, I don't think you really understood about our
being Linkletters. I mean you knew that we were a star's kids,
but you sent us to private schools where we mingled with other
celebrities' sons and daughters—my close friends were Vicki
Milland and Ann Widmark back then—and led a pretty sheltered
in-group life. But there was a difference. Vicki or Ann could go
into a department store and the clerk would never associate
either of them with Ray Milland or Richard Widmark; lots of
people are named Milland and Widmark.

"But just let me say 'Sharon Linkletter' and I was singled right
out and made to seem different."

Of course I understood that my kids might be recognized.
Perhaps I didn't fully appreciate the greater name recognition
or the real meaning of *different* to Sharon and the others.

"We all knew that you loved us but, well, you were always
so terribly busy and, honestly, you never were very demonstrative. I mean even with Mother. I can never remember seeing
you two touch or hug one another or anything like that. That's
changed, though, since Diane's death. I think you're much more
physical now."

All I can say is that you had two sisters and two brothers, young lady, so your mother and I must have touched, and even been "physical" occasionally during the past forty years.

"I think the first time that I knew what it was like to be a Linkletter was when you and Mother decided that private schools were isolating me from life and resolved to send me to a Los Angeles public school. I won't name the school but anyone who thinks that stars' kids lead some kind of wild, immoral existence should have been with me the first day I went to public school.

"I couldn't believe it. Kids were smoking pot in the playground (even the *idea* of pot was far-out then), there were washrooms set aside during certain hours by the kids for lesbians, and the language they used really freaked me out.

"Those kids were tough and determined not to be impressed by a name. I guess the teachers felt that they had to keep the kids' respect or something, because they were bad news too.

"I'll never forget my first roll call. We had to stand at our desks and speak our names in alphabetical order. When my turn came the teacher didn't even let me get it out. 'Sharon Linkletter,' he said, 'don't think that you're going to be treated differently from anyone else around here.'

"I nearly died, I was so embarrassed. I had never even thought of being treated differently. Well, it got worse. If I had to answer a homework question and made a mistake, somebody would crack, 'Kids say the darndest things,' from the back of the room. One day a boy hit me up for some money, saying that my father was such a big shot I could afford it. I lasted there for six months. Then you and Mother put me into Buckley, a private school, and I had no more problems."

Lois and I had the best of intentions sending Sharon to public school. We simply couldn't anticipate the pressures, and as soon as we realized our mistake, we rectified it. Her experience illustrates that show-business people have children who just want to be like everyone else but who are often trapped into bad situations. Sharon was also friendly with Liza Minnelli and Candy Bergen, who successfully capitalized on their parents' careers. My Diane was like Liza and Candy. She loved the spotlight and was on her way to becoming a celebrity in her own right. Jack, as you may know, had his own network television show when he was eighteen before deciding to go into business with me. But Sharon, Dawn, and Robert wanted their privacy, and now that they're adults, they have it. Unfortunately, when they were younger they were much more vulnerable.

I remember Robert telling me just recently that when he was in high school and the teacher put on a spelling bee he would always deliberately misspell the first word to avoid the hassle of students and teacher playing on his name every time he came back for another round. He would use a pseudonym to work in the summer, because he found out that as a Linkletter he would be either treated with embarrassing deference or stuck into some subbasement licking labels to show that his name didn't mean anything.

Robert's employment experience was duplicated at most of the children's schools, public or private. The teacher would either show favoritism or bend over backward to be impartial, which usually meant being unfair. I made it a point to meet most of the teachers to convey my desire that my daughters and sons were to be regarded as students, nothing more or less. I think that the personal contact helped, though it by no means solved the problem.

Despite Sharon's unfortunate experience, we did send some of the others to public schools with a minimum of trauma. Jack, an extrovert, graduated from Beverly Hills High, the families of whose students make up one of the two or three wealthiest such groups in the nation. I mention that fact because there is a tendency for rich kids not to be impressed by, or to intimidate, show-business children.

It would have been difficult, however, for anyone to intimidate Jack. Beverly Hills High is eighty-five percent Jewish; Jack ran for president of the student body as Jack Linkletterberg and very nearly won.

"I don't want you to think, Daddy, that I wasn't proud to be Sharon Linkletter. When I got a little older I could really enjoy it. I remember when I was carrying my first baby and was being attended by a top Beverly Hills obstetrician. I mean he was really big time, very sophisticated, traveled with the jet set, had luxurious offices, the works. Of course he knew me by my married name during the entire pregnancy.

"Well, came my time and everything went just fine. I was being wheeled out of the delivery room when I saw a nurse whisper something to Dr. Sophisticated. He leaned over me and said, 'Do you know whose waiting to see you on the other side of those doors?' I asked who. 'Art Linkletter,' he said. 'Why not?' I answered. 'He's my father.' The doctor did a long double take and swallowed. 'My Gawd,' he said. 'He's right here in person.'

"So being Sharon Linkletter has had its moments good and bad, with the good way, way ahead as far as I'm concerned."

No, the doctor didn't ask me for my autograph. But almost.

"I've gotten to know Mother and you much better since I've grown up. You were both gone so much in those days that we didn't have that much time to get acquainted. I know that Mother made a conscious decision to go with you on your travels because she felt safe leaving us with Edna. She was so much more than a governess to us and I know that you trusted her as one of the family. I honestly think you took Mother too much for granted because she was always ready to pack up and leave for one day or one week, anywhere that your personal appearances took you.

"Mother and I are so much closer, now. Like girlfriends rather than mother and daughter. As you know, she's great at sewing and needlepoint and since I make a lot of my own clothes I often ask her for advice. I don't have to make my own clothes but I'm too tight to pay $50.00 for a stupid tennis dress that I can make for $9.00 worth of material. I guess it must be inherited. The other day when you were away on a speaking tour back East I bought some material for a bikini; it cost me $1.50 and I was copying one that retails for $20.00. I took the bottom half over to show Mother and she looked at it for a few seconds and said, 'Where are you going to wear that?' I told her on the bottom, naturally. Then she said, 'No, I mean, out in public?' She's a doll."

What do you mean "inherited"?

"I nearly fell over one time when you were being interviewed by Merv Griffin. You're so smooth that you know what the host is going to ask before he asks it and you've got the answer ready so that it'll steer him toward the next question you want him to ask. So when he asked you 'What about Lois?' and you just sat there, I broke up. 'Lois?' you said. 'Yes, Lois,' Merv answered. 'Lois, your wife.' 'Well,' you said, 'she likes to work in the garden and does needlepoint.' Merv really had you and he knew it. 'Come on, Art,' he said. 'You've been married thirty-five years and that's all she's done?'

"It was the only time I've ever seen you at a loss for words and I'm using this to illustrate what I mean about taking her for granted. You could simply never imagine that someone would be interested in what Mother did."

She works in the garden, does needlepoint and keeps tabs on her children. That's the one I forgot.

Back at KGB, San Diego, the rewards and problems that I would face in the future were simply that, in the future. Even though I began to get a taste of what it meant to be a name, I still could not project that very local fame onto the larger canvas. My goals were limited only by my capacity to perceive them. In San Diego I looked to San Francisco as my stepping-stone to the big time. Matter of fact, San Francisco *was* the big time for a staff announcer on a small CBS affiliate. The bay city loomed as a challenge and a possible way station to Los Angeles, within whose environs was located a place called Hollywood, which offered the opportunity to be part of, and perhaps to conquer, the whole show-business world.

I was learning my trade quickly. When in November 1935 I got a $25 raise that boosted me to $175 a month, I finally persuaded Lois that she was in danger of losing out on a good thing. We were married at the Grace Lutheran Church, November 28, in a very simple ceremony with Gordy Samuel as best man and Lois's sister Jackie as maid of honor. After a brief honeymoon we moved into a small apartment. Within a few months I was named KGB's program director, no small honor for someone with my limited experience.

Clearly, I was on my way to station manager and who knows what after that. Which makes what I did a couple of months later a little difficult to explain even now. I quit to take a temporary job of indeterminate salary. And that started a series of quick, crazy leaps back and forth across the country that escalated my career to the point where I came to the notice of the United States government, which promptly indicted me.

Chapter Eight

An early religious upbringing contributed directly to my success in radio by forcing me to read cold. My father, as I've indicated, was a very pious man, so well versed in the Bible that at one time I was convinced he had committed it to memory. He always said grace before meals but was never satisfied with the perfunctory acknowledgments of other Christian households.

Dad Linkletter's table grace was a minisermon, a detailed thank-you to the Almighty citing chapter and verse to substantiate our appreciation of His bounty. Years later I liked to tell audiences that grace took so long at our table that I was sixteen before a warm meal crossed my lips. Although perhaps a slight exaggeration, the illustration does underline the atmosphere that prevailed during my youth. My father would gather us in the living room after dinner, hand me the Bible, and direct me to read long, involved passages containing biblical references and proper names that were especially tricky when seen for the first time.

I previously said that I could take no credit for my reading ability, but I must amend that and give a large assist to those evening devotional sessions, which delighted my father because his son appeared to take naturally to religious instruction, reading the Bible aloud as though inspired. No commercial ever gave me the slightest trouble after that early training. William Cowper's words "God moves in a mysterious way His wonders to perform" have had a special and sobering significance for me in many circumstances.

I have learned, sometimes through painful personal involvement, that one may undergo an experience that in retrospect was a preparation for life's future trials, without being aware of it at the time. During the period of the long grace and the reading "training" I was, of course, a preacher's kid or "PK" as my school chums dubbed me. Being a PK, the son of a man dedicated to the Lord's work, set me a little apart from the other boys as an object of curiosity and some awe. The PK, although he seemed physically the same as anyone else, was subjected to an imposed veneration that his fellows, being kids, tended to disparage. Sensing this need to prove myself as capable of sinning as anyone else, I tended to lead the pack on minor escapades designed to establish that the PK was anything but a sissy.

I was always first off the back end of the streetcar without paying the fare, and I could stroll casually through the corner grocery and emerge laden with enough candy and chewing gum to supply the entire gang for the whole day.

Small, boyish pranks you may say, smiling indulgently. But project that need of mine to the needs of my own children and a frightening analogy may be drawn. They too have been set apart from the group and, some more than others, have tried to prove their commonality with their peers. The impoverished son of an obscure preacher stole chewing gum; the wealthy daughter of a show-business millionaire took drugs. I realized after Diane's death how my own experiences on the streets gave me a better understanding of her needs and frustrations. The reaction is one of degree rather than kind. God does, indeed, move in a mysterious way.

Those reflections were far from the career-minded PK in San Diego. I had turned away from Bible reading and churchgoing both as a reaction against my youthful experience and because I was too busy with the materiality of my new vocation. Much later, after Diane died, I would experience another reversal, the last section of my personal religious trilogy; during that experience I came to relate my life more to the beliefs and philosophies of my father.

Even while I was going to college I rebelled against church attendance. Oh, I did belong to one church for a while. I loved to play basketball and was pretty good at it. But the most active league at that time was church sponsored; you had to belong to a church to play. Well, I thought about that and grudgingly took a friend's advice to go over to see the minister at the Brethren Church, a rather strict congregation that needed a good center. I rang the residence bell and the door opened to reveal an absolutely stunning teenage girl who asked me in and said that her father, the minister, would only be a few minutes. Would I mind waiting?

I decided on the spot, started at center the next Saturday afternoon, and was out necking with the daughter Saturday night. Remember necking? Not the best reason in the world to join a congregation, but my intentions were good and my technique kept me both on the court and in my friend's rumble seat with the minister's daughter for over a year.

I've often thought about my drift away from, then back to, my religious orientation. I've come to the conclusion that, for whatever reason, when someone is away from God and does very well in life, the better he does the more he tends to feel that he's making it on his own and doesn't need outside help of any kind. The more money I made, the more famous I got, and the more my family grew, the more I simply assumed that God had nothing to do with it, that I was progressing strictly on my own merits.

I've tried to follow the basic Christian morality of doing unto others as I would have them do unto me. I've never cheated anyone or knowingly caused anyone harm of any kind, not particularly because of any ecclesiastical direction, but because I thought this was the right way to live. I do see now, however, that it is very nearly impossible to separate the two; a Christian conscience almost automatically implies a belief in God and the hereafter. Although I have never consciously avoided evil and done right because I was afraid of the consequences in another life, I suppose that somewhere in the back of my mind my father's hellfire sermons took root and I felt that bad would be punished and good rewarded. Although those two concepts become increasingly blurred as our society grows more permissive, I firmly believe that anyone with a Christian upbringing can easily distinguish rightful from wrongful behavior and that this ability is the cornerstone of our American nation.

That doesn't mean that everyone has to read the Bible every day to become a decent, law-abiding citizen. Sometimes force-feeding religion doesn't have the desired effect because the information simply does not stick. Once on "People Are Funny" I noticed a small gold pin on the sweater of a little fellow I was interviewing. I asked him what it was for.

"Bible school," he replied.

"Does everyone who goes to Bible school get a pin?" I asked.

"No. Only boys who've gone four years."

"Well, isn't that nice. What's your favorite Bible story?"

"Humpty Dumpty."

I did a long double take as the audience roared. There were four years down the drain; nothing had really gotten through. And I think the same thing is true of much religious instruction; one really has to want to learn to become enthused by formal training. There is a place for those who do, but as far as I'm concerned, I regard myself as a beginning Christian, beholden to no particular sect or congregation. I believe that Christ lived and died for our sins, but everything beyond that is between me and my Christian conscience.

For example, I can't quite understand heaven as it is generally depicted by theologians. It sounds like the dullest place out of the world to me; I wouldn't want to be caught dead there. I've always thrived on work, struggle, the solving of entertainment and business problems; I cannot imagine spending eternity wandering around in some pastel environment listening to people sing and play the harp. I must believe that God in His infinite wisdom has figured out a different-strokes-for-different-folks situation.

I'm quite willing to concede that my finite mind can't envision what might await me in another world—even as children we couldn't conceive what it would be like to be grown up. Heaven has never been explained to my satisfaction by anyone in this world, but that may only mean that it is beyond rational conception. The unknown is always intriguing, although I must confess that its solution in this instance is perhaps the first challenge that I'm not in a great hurry to meet.

Billy Graham and I have spent many a long evening discussing Christianity and I'm the first to admit that I'm badly outclassed as far as background information goes. But there always comes a time in these friendly, stimulating chats when I'll ask him something like this: "Billy, do you believe that Jonah was really inside the whale's stomach?" He'll nod and tell me that if it's in the Bible it must be so. Now I have no quarrel with Billy or any other Christian believing that old Jonah was literally walking around in that big whale's belly, but I reserve the right to feel that perhaps the story was told as a parable rather than as an actual happening. I don't think that any Christian should become divided from any other Christian by what I call nonessentials.

I don't believe that it's essential or even particularly important that Billy Graham and I agree on biblical interpretation.

Look at what's happening to such great denominations as the Lutherans and the Roman Catholics; they are becoming more and more factionalized over relatively minor interpretations of dogma. I refuse to be drawn into that kind of often vitriolic, divisive argument, and I hope that Christianity's great strengths, the basics of right and wrong, of good and evil, will not be lost sight of amidst this lamentable in-fighting.

That is not to say that I think the various denominations and sects are not necessary to carry the Word to the faithful. People of varying social, economic, and cultural backgrounds need their Christianity served up on different procedural platters. It would be difficult to imagine Donald Coggan, the former archbishop of Canterbury, throwing his hands over his head at a Pentecostal revival meeting, joyously shouting "Hallelujah!" and skipping down the aisle to declare for Christ. That doesn't mean that the Anglicans are better or worse Christians than the Pentecostals; rather, that their approach is different.

I do feel that some Christian denominations place too much emphasis on a specific part of the religious service. For example, some Pentecostal sects emphasize the practice of speaking in the tongues—glossalalia—whereby a person who has come forward to receive Christ rises and utters a steady stream of sounds that are based on no known language and are indecipherable to the hearer. These sects believe that unless one gets to the stage where he can speak in tongues, he is not truly a born-again Christian. I feel that the ministers who preach that interpretation lose sight of the ultimate goals of Christian goodness and rightness, which have little to do with external manifestations.

There are occasions when speaking out or singing aloud can be effective and moving. I'll always remember one time when Danny Thomas asked me to substitute for him at a personal appearance that he very much wanted to make but that out-of-town contractual obligations superseded. Danny, as you may know, is the unofficial patron saint of St. Jude's Hospital. A very famous black architect had designed some new construction for St. Jude's without charge and Danny promised to return the favor anytime he could. The architect was a member of the Abyssinian Baptist Church and asked Danny if he would speak at a special service.

Danny called me, explained that his other obligation involved so many people that he couldn't get out of it, and asked me to go to this all-black congregation and speak in his place.

"You're the only one they'll accept, Art," he said. "They don't just want a star; they want one who they feel has a genuine empathy with them and what they believe in."

So I went and spoke to a packed church; when I finished there was a short period of silence, during which I wondered whether I had misread the whole situation. Then the minister came over to me, took my hand in both of his, and said simply, "We love you."

The entire congregation repeated the words, softly at first then with rising fervor until I stood there with tears trickling down my cheeks, overcome by that outpouring of love. Instead of feeling that I was doing a friend a favor, I became grateful to him for giving me the opportunity to be part of a mystical experience.

Now I couldn't see myself down there in the audience shouting "We love you" about someone else, nor could I see myself wet-eyed and speechless, yet there I was, feeling an emotion that I knew I would probably never again experience in a church, certainly not in any that I customarily attend.

In San Diego in 1935 philosophical observations on theological practice were not only far removed from my consciousness but, had they attempted to creep in, forbidden entrance. I was suffering from a religious overdose, so I threw myself more enthusiastically than most into my quest for material and professional goals. That search brought me into contact with someone who at first glance seemed a most unlikely partner.

Clyde Vandeburg to this day walks with a long, loping Colorado ranchhand's gait; he always looks as though he had just dismounted. When he first came to the KGB studios he was fresh from the wide-open spaces; one felt that if he tilted his head, the hayseed would trickle from his ear. Well, appearances are deceptive and never more so than in Clyde's case. His western heritage was legitimate, but somewhere on the trek to the Pacific Ocean he had honed a native intelligence to the point where he quickly got a cityslicker job representing the San Diego Chamber of Commerce as a public-relations adviser. One of his duties was writing and reading, on KGB, a weekly roundup of city happenings interspersed with historical vignettes.

As the duty announcer I was required only to introduce him and sign him off, between which I could go about my own business. But a chemistry quickly developed between us. I began improving sound effects, inventing ad-lib dialogue, and generally turning what, with all respect to Clyde, could have been a dull public-service broadcast into a minor dramatic triumph. For the first time in KGB's history the chamber of commerce's half-hour began getting fan mail, a circumstance roughly comparable to the Internal Revenue Service being complimented by the public for its efficient tax collection.

Naturally we had to do some remotes to top our own act, so we decided to capture the atmosphere of the world-famous San Diego Zoo by bringing animal sounds directly into our audience's living room. The animals, not quite grasping the exigencies of live radio or the honor being bestowed on them, often proved uncooperative, and more than one indignant squawk or startled roar was artificially induced because we were running out of air time.

When Clyde left the chamber of commerce to become advertising and promotion director of the California Pacific International Exposition, a tremendously ambitious undertaking for a city the size of San Diego, he asked me to come aboard as director of the public-address systems and radio spokesman for the world's fair. If you think I'm putting those two jobs in the inverse order of their importance you're wrong. Public-address systems were, in those days, the central nervous system of a big fair. Today with transistor radios and closed-circuit television supplementing the public-address system, large groups of people can be monitored and directed over wide areas very efficiently. But even now we need those speakers at strategic points to communicate with the crowds.

In 1935 the public-address system was in fact a miniature closed-circuit radio network, complete with its own studio, record library, and preestablished remote broadcast locations throughout the grounds. The fair network informed the visitors what big event was coming up, where an arriving celebrity could be seen, special attractions that had just been added, and where lost kids were being cared for, besides providing continuous music between announcements. It was just like a conventional radio station. I had a staff of announcers who covered the different pavilions, reporting everything from a massed-band recital to a hog-calling contest, which might be broadcast either to the crowd in that area or to the whole fair or over the radio, either local or network, or a combination of these choices.

My day might begin with an early morning visit with Alpha the Robot, who would answer my questions in a metallic voice and stand, move his arms, and sit on command (aided by a human accomplice inside him). It would be a fairwide broadcast from our television center, one of the exposition's wonders and located near the Ford Bowl, and there you could talk on the phone to someone in another part of the building and actually see his face on a blurry small screen. In the afternoon I might describe Sally Rand's fan dance for the local KGB audience, visit "Ripley's Believe It or Not" sideshow, cover a goat-judging contest in the agricultural hall, or, as I mentioned previously, bring in the Pacific Fleet. We might go full CBS network live to describe Franklin D. Roosevelt being greeted by California

Governor Frank Merriam and San Diego Mayor Percy Benbough.

Incidentally, I got Lois the first and only job she's had in her
life, selling loganberry juice at a little stand. She wasn't crazy
about it.

As you may imagine, the fair experience provided a series of
challenges that I would never have faced on a conventional radio
station. I had to be able to cover everything from an exhibition
of paintings in the Fine Arts Gallery to the gyrations of Flaming
Fanny and Golden Gulch Gertie, two belly dancers whose
shows, much to Clyde's delight, were closed periodically by the
San Diego Police only to be reopened with much hoopla and
suggestive narration by yours truly. Not only did I learn to
handle myself ad-lib in nearly every conceivable situation, but
I began to feel at ease with all kinds of people. I interviewed
everyone from Morton Downey to Chuck Bedell, the Hum-a-
Tune Man.

Bedell typified the freewheeling frontier spirit that made
America an exciting place in those days. Had he been born fifty
years earlier, he very likely would have been a patent-medicine
peddler or a riverboat gambling man. In 1935 he was a tall,
good-looking supersalesman con artist, one of the greatest pitch-
men on the circus and fair circuits. He set up a little umbrella-
topped table near the carnival midway and sold Hum-a-Tunes,
little waffle-shaped aluminum "instruments" that you put in your
mouth and "played." He could make it sound like Louis Arm-
strong's trumpet or Tommy Dorsey's trombone; he would then
sell it to you and it would sound exactly like hot wind blowing
through a piece of aluminum.

In between fairs Chuck would sell everything from special
spark-plug attachments that allegedly gave your car more power,
to those still flourishing shredding and slicing machines for the
kitchen. We were to meet again at the Texas and the San Francisco fairs and, most interestingly, while I was emceeing and
writing "People Are Funny." John Guedel and I were the head

writers in addition to producing the show and we were always hiring other writers and buying ideas. Once or twice a year Chuck Bedell would show up in Hollywood, broke, and sell me an idea. (His type had either a big bankroll or nothing.) He never came in without selling us at least one gag for a couple of hundred bucks, very good eating money in those days.

Chuck Bedell sold us the greatest stunt we ever used in the nineteen years "People Are Funny" was on the air—the idea of stealing someone's house. We bought a house sitting in the path of a planned freeway. It was due to be demolished in a year or so, but at the time it looked just like any other family residence in a quiet neighborhood. Then we set up a dummy real estate office so we could personally screen the applicants who answered a rental ad we put in the paper.

We finally rented the house to a young couple, the wife worked at the Broadway department store and her husband at what was then the Douglas Aircraft Company. We arranged with the Broadway management to run a fake contest in which customers supposedly voted for the most polite saleslady. The winner would receive an all-expense weekend vacation for two in San Francisco. Naturally, our renter won. Off the happy couple went by plane to enjoy themselves up north.

The moment they left, a big construction company we had hired began moving their house away. What we didn't know was that the couple owned a dog and had asked one of the wife's girlfriends to dog-sit while they were gone. The moving crew had barely got the jacks under the foundation when the window flew open and the poor woman began screaming for the police. Well, we got that straightened out, swore the friend to silence, and moved the house away.

When the couple returned from San Francisco they were met at the airport and told that, as an additional prize, they had audience tickets for the Art Linkletter "People Are Funny" program. They were very thrilled, because they knew we were booked up for months in advance; fans coming to Hollywood for a vacation would write for tickets well ahead of time.

We went on the air, live of course, and after a few warm-up jokes I asked if there was a local denizen in the audience who had been away from home for any length of time. Our renters' hands shot up. I invited them to the stage and was so pleased to learn that they had been away for the weekend, lived nearby, and had come directly to the broadcast. They were perfect, I explained, for a little experiment we wanted to carry out. Everyone, an hour or so after leaving home for a trip, begins wondering if he locked all the doors and windows, if the lights are turned out, the faucets off, and so forth. I think we had a list of about fifteen items and I asked them how they thought they would score in that situation.

They were very confident that they had forgotten none of the listed chores and eagerly accepted my offer to pay them fifty dollars for every one they had done right. So off we all went to the house. After a few turns around the block, they got out of the car to stare at an empty lot with some plumbing connections sticking up out of the ground. The house was gone and they, of course, began to get the idea that they were being had.

Back at the studio I told them that we would put them up at a first-class hotel and give them a big prize if they could find their house. It had not, I assured them, been destroyed and surely anyone could find something as big as a house. They might start, I suggested, at the police station Bureau of Missing Houses.

We carried on the gag for five weeks, flying them over different parts of the city, staging heavily publicized "sweeps" of residential areas, getting tremendous press coverage—and jumping our show into first place nationally.

The program originated from a theater just north of Hollywood and Vine with a big parking lot adjacent to it. We put up a huge carnival tent on the lot complete with flags, bunting, and signs announcing fortune tellers and horoscope readers; a real carny atmosphere. When our couple came back to the theater for their sixth appearance I asked them if they had noticed the tent next door and they said they had. I suggested that one of the fortune tellers inside might by gazing into a crystal ball give them a clue to the whereabouts of their house.

They were dubious but went next door, pushed aside the tent flap, and there, of course, was their house. It was truly a sensational stunt. Although our own writers worked out most of the details, it was essentially the Hum-a-Tune Man's idea, and we may never have done it had it not been for my exposition experience. The blow-off was that we gave the couple a rent-free year in a very nice home, plus lots of extras like clothes, furniture, and groceries. Everyone was happy and we had provided some good entertainment.

Back in San Diego the exposition closed after a very successful run, Clyde Vandeburg was offered a job in Texas, and to my pleasant surprise I was rehired as program director of KGB. Lois was happy that I was back in radio ready to resume my career after my little fling at the fair. Five months went by without much happening. I was learning all the time but the taste of adventure afforded by the fair made the daily routine of KGB appear dull. What many other young men my age would have given a great deal to attain, I accepted as a challenge met and overcome, and looked, as I do today, for new horizons. When I've finished a show or closed a business deal, the consummation is to me merely a prelude to the next experience.

Lois understands that now but in 1936 had some doubts. Then we owned one ancient car, rented an apartment, and had no money to speak of. Notwithstanding, she was just beginning to feel secure when I came home from the station one day and suggested that she should start packing. Clyde had phoned me from Dallas, where he was now promotion director of the Texas Centennial Exposition, and offered me the job of public-address system and radio director. We would once again be leaving a steady job with excellent though limited prospects for a temporary shot in unfamiliar territory.

But Lois was game and just naturally assumed that the money involved would more than compensate for quitting my job and spending our savings to drive to Dallas. We were heading east along what is now Interstate 80 and, as I recall, had just gone through El Centro when Lois popped the question.

"Salary, honey?" I answered. "Gosh, I didn't think to ask."

We drove in silence for some time, but she never could stay mad at me for very long. Besides, I knew that she was just as excited as I at the prospect of our new adventure. So, when we had to borrow money from Clyde to pay our first week's rent in Dallas, she just took it in stride.

In retrospect, I can offer no rational explanation for making that move to Dallas; nothing more than an instinctive feeling that it might take me, however indirectly, out of a deepening rut in San Diego. And I was right. The road to Dallas would eventually lead to fame and fortune—but not before a couple of near disasters along the way.

Reverend Rueban John Linkletter –
Baptist Evangelist

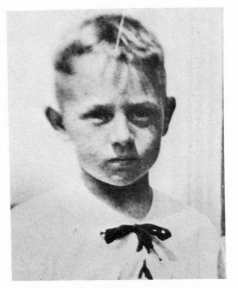

Earnest young Art
going into First Grade

All-Conference Center Captain Linkletter and his championship team-mates – 1934

(1935) Radio Director (and M.C.) of the San Diego World's Fair in Balboa Park

When I still thought of myself as a leading man!

Someone's idea of a "Glamour" shot

A "Fun Magazine" shot of a non-existent job!

Five Little Links

Santa Claus Lane Parade on Hollywood Boulevard 1955

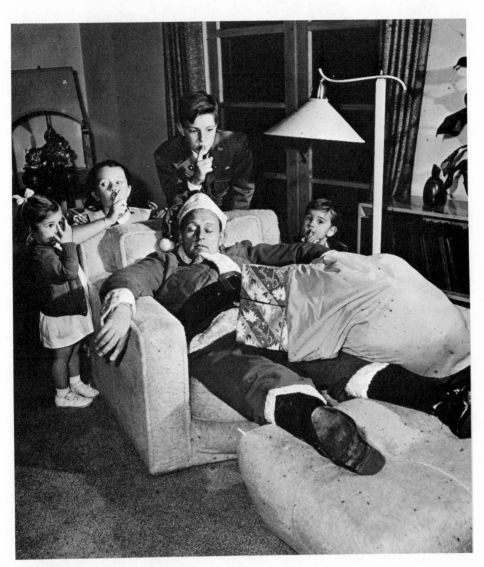

Family Reunion at Christmas 1955

Art goes "Australia"

Art & Groucho with Producer-Partner John Guedel

Feeding the Reagan's early on!

Two of the 5 Link's who decided on
show business careers, Jack and Diane

Five of the seven grandchildren with Grandpa Art (About 1970)

Chapter Nine

I conducted my first, and last, choir in Dallas.

An exposition or world's fair thrives on publicity and Clyde Vandeburg had a stunt awaiting me that taxed my mental and physical resources almost to the limit. He had arranged with the state director of education, Florenz Eddington, up for reelection and seeking a public forum, to act as the Pied Piper of the Texas Centennial Exposition in Dallas.

Clyde's plan was as simple in concept as it was colossal in execution. The Gulf Oil Company, heavy backers of the exposition, had a fleet of soundtrucks fanned out across the state trumpeting the fair's praises. With Eddington's cooperation Clyde selected five or six recorded songs of a stirring or patriotic nature, distributed copies to every school in Texas, and had the students learn to sing the songs as a class or school project.

Individual schools then assembled at local stadiums. With the

Gulf trucks' assistance, they formed larger choruses until the final ensemble would be a 50,000 voice choral group sent on an all-expenses-paid trip to the Dallas exposition. There, in one magnificent performance, "The Eyes of Texas" and similar choice selections would be heard not only in the Cotton Bowl, located in the center of the fairgrounds, but, courtesy of the NBC Radio Network, for a half-hour across the entire country.

Before we knew it some 78,000 schoolchildren were in competition in the state. Clyde and I began to get nervous. It looked as though we would have an overnight influx of some 50,000 children, teachers and parents utilizing the already overextended Dallas accommodation facilities. We mobilized the National Guard, the Boy Scouts, the Red Cross, and the YMCA, and they provided cots and field kitchens. NBC increased its time to a full hour. It soon became apparent that the eyes of the nation were on Texas and the Dallas exposition.

As the fateful day approached, the heat was on us, literally and figuratively. We had gotten the feeding and sleeping arrangements organized during a steadily climbing southern Texas hot spell, which worried the NBC engineers. They had never set up microphones to transmit 50,000 massed voices through their equipment, and they were fretful that the first ringing notes of "The Eyes of Texas" would blow us right off the air. Would sensitive microphones accept that outpouring of sound, or would some sort of overload cause superhot vacuum tubes to fail? No one really knew as carpenters erected a large podium on the Cotton Bowl field so that the choral conductor, an ancient and venerated music teacher from a rural Texas school, could be easily seen by the 47,000 children and 20,000 adults we now knew for certain would be attending.

Our air time was from ten to eleven o'clock in the morning, uncomfortably close to high noon on a very muggy ninety-eight-degree June day. NBC had sent out an announcer from New York to handle the broadcast and he appeared hatless and sweating in the 9:30 A.M. prebroadcast humidity. We had rigged a special baton for the conductor, a five-foot white stick with rhine-stones stuck to one end for high visibility. I waited at one side for my big moment, introducing Mr. Eddington to the country and, not so incidentally, to his Texas constituency and thanking him, all just before network sign-on.

We went on the air without a hitch. The conductor led the great choir through its first number—heard clearly without ra-dios by the employees of the Texas State Building, a quarter-mile away. The NBC announcer introduced the second, and the third number. He delivered the half-hour station break, paused while the local stations gave their call letters, then launched the last half of the program.

By now the heat was intense and I could see young singers dropping here and there, to be attended quickly by our well-organized first-aid squads. The maestro stood on the podium, raised his hands, waggled his baton, and passed out. I've heard that people react in an emergency instinctively, without being conscious of the long odds that might be against them, because of the adrenalin flow at that moment. Out of the corner of my eye I saw Clyde and some assistants dragging the prostrate vir-tuoso off the podium. I stepped quickly forward and, before I fully realized what I was doing, grasped the baton and was giving the downbeat for the next song.

It remains in my memory as a tribute to the sturdy sons and daughters of the Lone Star State that they came in on cue and translated my uncertain gestures into full-voiced, beautiful har-mony. Even so, the situation was rapidly deteriorating. Heat exhaustion began to fell dozens of singers. I motioned for the decimated ranks to close up nearer to the microphones.

Thinking ahead, I hoped that the announcer would anticipate my problem and arrange to introduce the education director, who stood, unruffled by the savage heat, waiting for his big moment. The echoes of the last song died away and I turned, nearly exhausted, to see the announcer swaying dizzily on the platform only to fall backward and disappear over the edge even as Mr. Eddington, undaunted, mounted the steps to clinch his coming election.

I ran back to the microphone, aware that only silence was filling precious seconds of network air. Melting under the Dallas sun, I profusely thanked Mr. Eddington for assembling this vast chorus and assured him that his name would go down in history as the first music teacher from a modest Texas school to produce such an incredible choral offering.

The sequence of events right after that remain blurred in my memory, probably with good reason. We had intended to honor the music teacher for his outstanding choral work after the program, but the heat and the pressure of my baton waving had gotten to me. Clyde told me later that the education director's face, free of any sign of the hot sun till then, turned a tomato red and that he had been unable to say anything before the engineer drew a finger sharply across his throat signaling that we were off the air. But all turned out well because the name Eddington had gone over the airwaves loud and clear; my error actually resulted in calling greater attention to our distinguished patron, a fact that was later substantiated by his landslide victory at the polls.

Gradually, like any other performing talent, mine was being tested and fine-tuned along the way. I was learning, Florenz Eddington notwithstanding, that I was up to most situations that might confront someone who was making a career of extemporaneous broadcasting. Even the most carefully planned situations could go completely awry and my particular personality equipped me to deal with the unexpected in a professional manner.

Quite often the odds on the unexpected can be considerably shortened by a little judicious fakery. Opening day of the San Diego Exposition serves as an excellent illustration of how preplanning can create the illusion of a happening. If you remember that opening, you will now learn for the first time what the network radio audience really heard on that momentous day whose heroics included the arrival of the phantom Pacific Fleet.

The actual opening of the front gates was to take place in the morning, and we had a real blockbuster idea designed to get us international attention, an ambitious notion in those days. The French liner *Normandie*, then the most luxurious passenger liner afloat, was beginning its maiden voyage off the French coast. As a salute from the Old World to the New, the captain was scheduled to blow the ship's whistle, the sound to be carried by short wave across the Atlantic, then over the network to the fairgrounds. There, through unspecified electrical devices, the whistle would activate the bells set in place in Mission San Diego by Father Junipero Serra, its founder, in 1769. The ringing bells would then signal President Franklin Roosevelt in the White House to press a button on his desk to start up the front gate mechanism, officially opening the fair.

I took on what seemed the simplest task first—lining up some bells. After visiting several missions up and down the coast (most, incidentally, founded by the peripatetic Father Serra), I realized that what bells existed were immovable, or cracked, or, if in ringing condition, very likely to come across the microphone like old brass spittoons being kicked by someone's boot. So I went down to the Ratliff Ballroom, a popular dancing spot on Broadway, and borrowed a low-C chime from the band's drummer.

Came opening day, I took the network cue, and announced: "In a salute from the Old World to the New we will hear direct from the luxury liner *Normandie* steaming out into the Atlantic on her maiden voyage, the stirring sound of her ship's whistle signaling the opening of the California Pacific International Exposition!"

Nothing.

"In a salute from the Old World to the New. . . ." I went through it again, to be greeted by the crackling of a short-wave transmitter but no whistle. Then, with millions of people straining to hear the *Normandie*'s signal, came the voice of my engineer sitting out of sight at his console right behind the reviewing stand. "Anybody hear the damn whistle?" he inquired, eyes glued to his motionless potentiometer indicators.

Fortunately, right on top of his words the *Normandie* came through; then the mission bells sounded—really my sound-effects man back in the studio whacking away at the borrowed chime—and they alerted the President to push the button that opened the front gates.

There is a lot to be said for the maxim "What you don't know won't hurt you." We had a big mail response to that broadcast, most of it ignoring our *Normandie* feat but praising us for reviving the wonderful mission bells that so many listeners had heard in their youth but had never hoped to hear again with such fidelity.

My choice of the Ratliff Ballroom from which to borrow that chime was far from accidental. The Ratliff was at least partially responsible for a marriage that has brought me a great deal of happiness these past forty-plus years.

I was a skinny, pimply-faced kid in high school, one year ahead of my class and smaller than my fellow students. I matured quickly during my hobo days, putting on height and weight, but in my middle teens I never really got to play basketball or hang around with the big guys and soon found that I was having trouble competing for the attention of the more desirable young ladies. In those days the Ratliff was a dime-a-dance hall and I started frequenting the place for two reasons: the girls *had* to dance with me and by learning to dance well, I figured I would have more of a chance in the romance department.

This book could well be dedicated to those unsung heroines of the Ratliff who had their feet stepped on and shins kicked by an awkward, stumbling kid who kept coming up with strips of dance tickets that had to be honored. But I learned quickly and soon found I had a natural aptitude with my feet that gradually drew the notice of the comelier coeds, who condescendingly at first, then with rising enthusiasm permitted themselves to be swept around and, as time went by, off the floor. To this day, I say it without false modesty, I am one hell of a ballroom dancer.

The dance floor is what drew Lois and me together originally. She was a terrific dancer and soon began to appreciate my own talents. We went to every place where we could dance for nothing—street dances, fraternal dances, or any public dances where we could work our way past the ticket taker. Dancing opened up a whole social world for me and, as it turned out, helped me select a life partner as well. Those early days, before I went to college or started in radio, were lots of fun, but a different kind of fun, more carefree than what I would experience later when I brought in an imaginary fleet of warships or, to pick up our story at the Dallas exposition, I had to describe a nonexistent meteor bursting from the heavens to explode in a great sheet of flame over the crowded fairgrounds.

Clyde and I had hired a local astronomer and started planting stories in the daily papers regarding a meteor reportedly on a collision course with earth. At first the items attracted little notice; soon, however, the astronomer divulged more specifics, even isolating the great state of Texas as the probable point of contact. This news was greeted with scorn or good-natured disbelief for the most part, but when the learned man concluded that the mighty meteor would undoubtedly enter our atmosphere near Dallas and explode right smack over the fairgrounds on June 6, our opening night, the howls of derision could be heard from Amarillo to Houston. The wire services had picked up the story and we were getting a Texas-size hee-haw.

Clyde was delighted and I was learning fast. The disbelievers, he assured me, would come in droves, afraid that the meteor might be for real. The important thing now was to arrange for a meteor that would do justice to our publicity budget and, we hoped, make the front page of every newspaper in the country. First we arranged with a fighter pilot—pursuit pilot at that time—from nearby Love Field to fly our "meteor." Then we enlisted the aid of General Electric and Eastman Kodak, two fair exhibitors, to attach a battery of rockets to its wings and mount a huge bank of high-powered photoflash bulbs atop the Ford Tower, the fair's tallest structure.

The rockets, fired in sequence from the cockpit, would produce an impressive meteor tail and the photoflash bank would "explode" for several seconds of one billion candlepower of illumination. I took over the sound effects, using greatly amplified drums, wind machines, and long sheets of tin that, when vibrated from either end in a continuous ripple motion, emitted an ear-bursting cacophony guaranteed to make a lasting impression on even the most jaundiced out-of-state newsmen. Our amplifying system contained enough power to operate several standard radio stations. By opening night we were ready to blow everyone's mind.

Radio was the key to getting our message across, so I went full NBC network to describe the turnaway crowds at the world's greatest exposition as well as the wonders within. As I spoke I could hear the sound of our meteor droning in circles above us at 16,000 feet, its pilot watching, we hoped, the concealed light that we put on the Ford Tower to serve as his target.

Everything was coordinated for the meteor's arrival at 8:25 P.M. By 8:20 I was working the crowd, the radio audience, and myself into a frenzy of anticipation.

"No one knows exactly what will happen," I announced tersely, little realizing the accuracy of my prediction. "This flaming visitor from another world may light up half the continent as it explodes in our atmosphere. Or it may pass far above us, to plunge harmlessly into the Gulf of Mexico. [Dramatic pause.] In just sixty seconds we should know the answer."

I had millions of believers in that last minute as I heard the characteristic whine of the open-cockpit biplane going into its dive directly overhead. Our pilot fired the first rocket and its flaming tail seemed to appear from nowhere, completely obscuring the plane and creating a sensational effect.

My voice rose as I began describing the incredible event. The astronomer's predictions had been true! We were witnessing the actual approach of a body from outer space, its fiery tail a flaming stream as it plunged closer to the Dallas exposition.

Abruptly, as the first rocket died, all was darkness overhead. The pilot later explained that he had frantically jiggled all the firing switches, but that our tail must have shorted out. The darkness didn't slow me down. As the crowd strained to see what was happening, the radio audience was treated to a description—second to none, if I do say so myself—of a fiery meteor entering our atmosphere.

I was listening as the plane kept up its screaming dive, timing my "eyewitness" account to coincide with the enormous "fireball" that would erupt from the Ford Tower as the meteor "exploded," bringing my audience up to date on actual events. The plane pulled out of its dive and the engineers fired the rows of photoflash bulbs on cue. If you have ever been set to take a flash picture only to have the bulb fail to go off, just multiply that ten thousand times and you get a faint idea of how I felt at that moment. Two or three of the bulbs went off with sick little pops, providing about enough light to take a family portrait in a small room. At that moment the sound effects let go, filling the air with rumbling, ear-piercing sounds that would have done credit to a large earthquake. The sound, of course, went out over the air, and that was all I needed.

"The meteor has just exploded with an incredible blaze of light," I reported, "right over the packed fairgrounds. The Dallas exposition has been opened by a blinding signal from space and the hundreds of thousands of people gathered here are standing in awestruck silence."

That last part was true. They were wondering what the devil was going on. This was before transistor radios, but my voice was carried over our entire fair-speaker network and I talked for an additional three or four minutes, taking us right up to our network sign-off at 8:29:30. In the glass control booth I could see Clyde, the engineers, and the sound men cavorting around gleefully in tribute to my performance. In many ways it beat bringing the fleet into San Diego Bay, for it demanded far more enthusiasm and spontaneity.

Not all of my broadcast experience in Dallas was so spectacular. Especially my coverage of Clyde's hog-calling contest, one of our most successful San Diego promotions. We could only get local radio time, the networks feeling that New York, Chicago, and Los Angeles were not quite ready for this bit of Americana.

Just before air time at a livestock shed I was greeted by an unbelievable din; the hog callers were testing their range and tone and fifty or so resentful porkers were responding with indignant squeals and grunts. That kind of natural sound effect makes for great radio so I signed on with the feeling that this was going to be a breeze, no imaginary scenes to describe or atmosphere to create.

All went well until one big, tusked boar, which must have weighed over three hundred pounds, decided that his dignity had been assaulted. He promptly flopped over onto his side, seemingly oblivious to the hoarse entreaties of his human caller. Sensing rising drama, I climbed over a gate to get closer to the action. The hog, acknowledging the calls with perfunctory grunts, was driving the caller to greater and greater histrionic heights.

The hog raised his head and eyed me appraisingly as I pointed my metal mike at him. Would this giant swine, I asked my radio audience breathlessly, this monster porker respond to the now frantic entreaties of his master? Maybe not to his master but he decided that *my* presence was offensive and suddenly displaying amazing agility, was on his feet and rushing me. Before I could move, my right pant leg was gone from the knee down, flapping wildly on a boar tusk. No one clocked me but I think the *Guinness Book of World Records* could have created a new category—fastest time for a radio announcer out of a pigpen. And it didn't do my ego any good to look back, panting, from the top of the gate and see that big hog settling placidly down on his side with part of my pants caressing his snout. I guess you might call that incident the first adverse critical evaluation of my work.

Even as we kept things hopping in Dallas new horizons were beckoning Clyde Vandeburg and me. Our fame as a team had spread. San Francisco, anxious to lure commerce and tourists, asked us to come there to help establish the biggest fair yet, the Golden Gate International Exposition. Clyde went first, leaving me in charge of exploitation and publicity in Dallas. As soon as my services were no longer needed, Lois and I joined him in San Francisco. The new fair was to be located on the site of the Yerba Linda shoals, just north of Yerba Buena Island, known as Goat Island by San Franciscans, and the middle point of the $80,000,000 San Francisco Bay Bridge linking the city with Oakland. A massive dredging operation would convert the shoals into solid ground, christened Treasure Island, a magic entertainment place about which, as radio director, I would send out the good word far and wide.

The "Pageant of the Pacific," as Clyde promptly dubbed it, was still in the construction stage—although we were getting thousands of dollars' worth of free air time by extolling its largely imagined virtues—when two important events occurred in my life: Lois gave birth to Jack on November 20, 1937, just a couple of weeks before our second anniversary, and Harris Connick, the fair's general manager, launched my freelance career by firing me for insubordination.

Chapter Ten

What's in a name? A great deal if you happen to be running an international exposition. Two things are dear to every fair director's heart: a smashing, sensational, media-saturated opening day, and for everything a name that will fit into a one-column headline.

With one year to go and the "fairgrounds" still silt on the bottom of the bay, we had to take advantage of every public-relations opportunity, so we mounted a nationwide contest to name the midway, with the prize an all-expense-paid trip to the fair. The midway was to play an important part in our overall promotion; it was essential that it have a name that was snappy, memorable, and reasonably short. A staff member promptly submitted "Mud," and I believe he has not been heard from since.

"Treasure Island" had caught on quickly with the public and we hoped that its thinking would follow along the same general lines of bountiful good fortune and fun. Like so many other things in the promotional field, the contest was not what it appeared to be. Clyde and I had our hearts set on a name for the midway that we thought would be a natural: Barbary Coast. It suggested to us the swashbuckling, riotous, carefree days of the 1849 gold rush and seemed to typify the fair spirit we were trying to project. We felt that enough contestants would submit that name to make it the logical choice.

As brash outsiders we did not take into account the nature of the genus San Franciscan, an insular, somewhat provincial biped who for the most part associated the Barbary Coast with every imaginable sordid vice. What seemed to us reminiscent of a romantic era remained, to the old-line families, a totally unacceptable memory; the very name "Barbary Coast" raised a stench in the nostrils of the Nob Hill elite, whose approval we desperately needed.

Even though our strategy worked—the name "Barbary Coast" was submitted from nearly all forty-eight states—San Franciscans were doing the judging. After conscientiously considering more than 400,000 names, the chairman of the judging committee informed us that a selection had been made.

We set up a news conference and the chairman, who with an unexpected flair for drama had refused to tell us his decision, went into a long preamble about different names and, finally, got to the point.

"I now take pleasure," he declared, "to announce the winning name as unanimously selected." Clyde and I exchanged glances that said, "I'll bet."

"Henceforth," the civic leader continued, "that brilliant strip of gaiety on top of Treasure Island will be known to one and all as . . . the Gayway! I give you, ladies and gentlemen, the Gayway and its attendant slogan Forty Acres of Fun."

Well, it really wasn't all that bad. Today, of course, the homosexual organizations would proclaim a day of national rejoicing and we would be stuck with a double entendre that might well get us more publicity than we desired. In those days of relative innocence a generation ago, we had a few inside snickers; the name didn't seem to us to have the necessary spark but we could live with it. I immediately began extolling its virtues but not, it turned out, to everyone's satisfaction.

"Everyone" in the day-to-day operation of the Golden Gate International Exposition meant a gentleman named Harris DeHaven Connick, who inadvertently launched me on a lucrative, rewarding career. As I've mentioned, both Clyde and I were regarded as outsiders in the framework of the local establishment. I was a special target because I was still a kid; although I had two world fairs under my belt and had to be acknowledged as a professional, I came in to take a plum job as radio director at a time when radio played an extremely important role in publicity and promotion. Hollywood was just then catching up to San Francisco as the West Coast radio center; it would soon surpass the bay city, but at that time local radio experts could still look down their noses when they were pointed south.

Connick had impeccable fair credentials. He had run the Panama Pacific Fair in 1915, and, in his late sixties, had been called in as a kind of elder statesman cum troubleshooter for the 1938 exposition. He took his job seriously, too seriously perhaps. For reasons that escape me to this day, he decided that no decent San Francisco fair could be promoted by barbarians from places like Colorado and San Diego. Remember, all we had to work with was a fleet of dredges tossing river-bottom silt up into a big pile in the bay, yet Connick, crusty and short-tempered, was never satisfied with our efforts.

He called me to his office one day and chewed me out. "Mr. Linkletter," he began with the formality of a judge imposing the maximum penalty, "I regret to say that in my opinion your work has been dull, without imagination, and more or less useless."

I began to suspect that he was displeased with my performance. We had all been casting about for a surefire opening-day gimmick. Clyde and I had arranged for Richard Halliburton, the famous author, to go to China, purchase a large junk, then sail back to arrive at the Golden Gate on opening day. It was a good stunt, which would have day-to-day promotional value while the world followed Halliburton's progress. As I stood in Connick's office (he never did ask me to sit down) the author was on his way to China, where he eventually outfitted a junk, sailed for San Francisco, and was lost at sea. But that was in the lamentable future.

Harris Connick told me in very direct language what he thought of the whole idea. I got hot but managed to limit my reply to a question: What did *he* have in mind for opening day?

"The obvious, Mr. Linkletter," he said patronizingly, "the obvious." He waved his hand toward a window overlooking the Golden Gate Bridge. "See those suspension cables?" he asked.

"Yes."

"Ever *hear* those cables?"

"Yes, I have." The cables made a sound when the ocean wind hit them.

"That is music you hear, Mr. Linkletter," Connick said, smiling condescendingly. "Each cable has a different tension that produces its own note. All you have to do is pick out the eight notes on the scale, if you know them, and put a microphone on each one."

"And then?" I asked numbly.

"You run wires from the microphones to a keyboard console and, on opening day, you get someone like Artur Rubinstein to sit down and play "California Here I Come" on the world's largest aeolian harp!" He beamed as he pictured the scene in his mind. "What do you think of *that*?" he demanded.

My answer was almost involuntary. "Mr. Connick," I said, "I think you're nuts."

The smile disappeared. "And I *know*, Mr. Linkletter," he said, "that you're fired."

At home Lois looked up in surprise as I walked in the door. "You're early," she said.

"I've got great news," I said.

"What is it?"

For the last couple of years I had been explaining that all this temporary work, traveling back and forth across the country for very little money, had been a training period, an apprenticeship that was preparing me for the big time. When I had learned my craft to my satisfaction, I had assured her, I was going out on my own to find both fame and fortune.

"I've decided the time has come to make it big," I announced grandly.

"What do you mean?"

"I'm going freelance."

"What about your job?" Women are so literal-minded.

"My imagination has been stifled long enough."

"You got fired."

"Just before I was going to resign."

I wasn't exactly kidding. Although the timing was a trifle abrupt, the truth was that I had been getting restless and was constantly seeing opportunities to make money on the side. In San Diego and Dallas I had always picked up extra cash emceeing shows or writing publicity for the exhibitors, but now, in San Francisco, I went out to sell my services independently on a full-time basis.

I knew the coming fair schedule intimately and lost no time contacting the exhibitors one by one. I reminded them of their approaching promotional dates and offered my services as what we now call a packager, someone who puts all the talent and support people together, then sells them to the sponsor as a complete show.

Although I was no longer on the exposition staff, I had left an indelible imprint on the format that stood me in good stead when I began soliciting private accounts. Based on the great success of the Cavalcade stage productions in San Diego and Dallas, I had been asked to write and coproduce the *Cavalcade of the Golden West*, a truly impressive extravaganza featuring on stage, among other things, an actual cattle drive with cowboys and Indians, and re-creations of the 1906 earthquake and fire, and the meeting of the Central Pacific and the Union Pacific trains at historic Promontory Point, near Ogden, Utah, on May 10, 1869, when a gold spike driven into the final tie linked the East and the West by rail.

A cow actually gave birth on stage during one performance.

I wanted to add realism to the frightening earthquake special effects by mounting the audience seats over long rows of hydraulic jacks, which would cause the whole place to buck up and down, but the insurance companies wouldn't go for it; they said the possibility of people falling down or having heart attacks was too great a risk. Today there is a sound technique that gives the illusion of violent earth movement in a theater. I guess I was a little ahead of my time.

I was fired two weeks before the fair opened and two weeks after the opening I was making more money than the fair's president. Beginning with my first network radio account, the Roma Wine Company, which sponsored "World's Fair Party"—a live audience-participation half-hour from the auditorium stage of the Food and Beverage Building over the entire CBS–Don Lee western network every Saturday night—I spread to so many exhibitors over the fairgrounds that I jumped my earnings from $300 to $2,000 a month, a very respectable sum at that time.

"World's Fair Party" was the forerunner of "People Are Funny" and "House Party." It was the first real test of my ability to sustain a show for a half-hour by talking to people and it wasn't long before I was initiated into the perils of my newly discovered broadcast form.

Fair visitors soon got to know about the broadcast so we always had more than enough honeymooners, golden-wedding celebrants, people all the way from you-name-it, to keep the show fresh and lively. I was beginning to feel my broadcast oats; obviously spontaneity was one of the major reasons for the show's and my rising popularity. One night I was interviewing a young couple who were planning to be married the following week. "Well," I suggested, "why not come back here next Saturday night to be married right here on stage with millions of people listening in?"

The young couple loved the idea, the audience roared its approval, and I got carried away. As we signed off I said something like, "Now don't forget, next week this fine young couple will return to the Roma Wine Exhibit to consummate their marriage right here on stage!"

It's easy, when you're ad-libbing, to hear the words slide out of your mouth even as you realize that you're not saying exactly what you mean. My sponsor called to point out that in marriage the ceremony and consummation were two entirely different acts, just in case I didn't know. As I recall, the next Saturday night we took a rating and our simple marriage ceremony swamped all the opposing stations; apparently the audience wasn't sure if I knew the difference, either.

When the fair closed I found myself in a very good position as a radio personality. A San Franciscan for three years, I was now accepted and well known because of my work in connection with the fair. I began signing up local advertisers. The format of my shows required very little overhead and appealed to merchants with limited budgets; I was soon doing twenty-one broadcasts a week, varying in length from five minutes to a half-hour, over five radio stations.

My easygoing, off-the-cuff approach to programming was paying off. For example, I sold a weekly half-hour show called "Who's Dancing Tonight?" to a local jeweler. Every Saturday night I set up in the lobby of the St. Francis Hotel, checked with the maître d' to see who was having special birthday or other celebrations in the hotel that evening, then kidded with selected guests for half an hour. That was it. But it became the highest-rated local show on the air and I knew for certain, if I'd ever had any doubts, that a sponsor could drop me and my microphone into the middle of a crowd anywhere and I could provide entertainment by simply encouraging folks to be themselves. It was a good feeling, one that any professional—actor, pianist, baseball pitcher, or quarterback—experiences when he or she has mastered a skill.

No matter how confident one is of his abilities, experience is the only teacher that gives him the poise to anticipate a bad move and avoid it in a split second. And, I'm convinced, the only way to recognize potential bad moves is to make a few of your own.

I was doing a show called "Market Street Happenings" for Gallenkamp Shoes during which I roamed one of San Francisco's main thoroughfares and randomly engaged passersby in conversation. One day I heard a siren coming—a real bonus to a man-in-the-street interviewer—and began describing how cars pulled over and people ran for the sidewalk as an ambulance daringly snaked through seemingly impassable traffic. As it roared by I described its receding flashing red lights and said, "There it goes," adding, after a brief pause, "followed by a carload of lawyers."

I was young. The way the local bar association came down on my sponsor you'd think that lawyers were overly sensitive about the subject. I suggested that next time I would amend my description to "followed by a carload of *Oakland* lawyers," but was given to understand that, by and large, the law is no place for levity.

Gallenkamp stayed with me as a sponsor but other unrehearsed hilarity cost me money. It is traditional, almost mandatory, in the radio business—more then than now because today's announcers tend to be less highly trained—for experienced microphone men to "break up" newer recruits, especially in the more competitive metropolitan cities. In the old days a man who worked in San Francisco had cut his teeth on a number of smaller stations and was expected to be able to withstand an initiation at the hands of his fellows.

As a freelance who was making considerably more money than the salaried staff announcers, I was a particularly enticing target. Actually, I should have known what to expect. One day back in San Diego I was on the air for the P. J. Benbough Funeral Parlor reading public-service announcements and inviting the listeners to use my client's facilities. While I was reading the commercial part of the program, a twin-piano team that I hired for another show—"Keyboard Varieties," for Breast o' Chicken Tuna—came into the studio. The senior member produced a box of matches, lighted one, and ceremoniously handed it to his buddy, who promptly ignited one corner of the script I was holding.

Now that was accepted, if unsettling, behavior. The unwritten rule had it that anything could be perpetrated against the guy on the air so long as it was still possible for him to read his copy. One could not, for example, grab the copy out of an announcer's hand and throw it away or tear it, for then he would have to stop reading. But otherwise, he was fair game. Well, I put out the fire without missing a beat, but my attention was distracted and I had trouble keeping my voice steady.

Then one partner pulled out the little well that caught excess water from the water cooler and sat in it. I was just going into the last few sentences and was, as I recall, reading, "The funeral services at the P. J. Benbough Funeral Parlor include mauso-leum [the pianist stood up and sat down again so that water from his soaked backside splashed on the floor], interment [I couldn't control a snicker], and [the final words came out in a burst of uproarious laughter] CREMATION FACILITIES!"

I lost the account, but the experience stood me in good stead in San Francisco, where one day during a maternity-clothes commercial a rotund studio musician (musicians tend to be a little squirrelly about these things) disrobed completely in front of me without affecting my, ah, delivery. An event that appears to be only mildly amusing in casual conversation becomes much more humorous when the situation forbids laughter. Indeed, such a situation may produce an overwhelming compulsion to react, and even exaggerated histrionics. A result is a special kind of in-comedy, about which the public is generally unaware.

Because I have a highly developed sense of humor that reacts strongly to the ridiculous, I tended to appreciate the off-microphone antics more than most and had consciously to gain control of myself when those shenanigans were aimed at me. Because I had to, I mastered a natural tendency to laugh on the wrong occasions and that seemingly minor accomplishment reflects, in microcosm, my whole life pattern.

In a very real sense I have always been in competition with myself. I have never had a life goal in the usual context of wanting to be owner of a radio station or to make ten million dollars. My only goal has been to be better, to go on to a new challenge. Getting a higher rating, landing a new sponsor, or concluding a multi-million-dollar business deal has always served as a stimulus to go on to something else. The moment an immediate goal is reached, it ceases to interest me; I look only to the future and to whatever risks and, I hope, triumphs lie ahead.

Friends ask me why I continue to be so active in business, why I travel around the country making close to two hundred personal appearances per year for substantial fees. "You don't need the money" would sum up an attitude that, though well meaning, completely misses the point. The money is no longer the prime motivating factor. The challenge is the thing. Do I have something to offer, in business or the entertainment field, that people want badly enough to pay for? For that, in the final analysis, is the mark of the truly successful professional. Anyone can follow the stock market on paper as a risk-free pastime, or write only for their own reading pleasure, or talk a good story into a home tape cassette, but only those who are prepared to take the heat of the commercial marketplace can really test themselves and discover their true worth.

There are arenas that I now choose not to enter. I will no longer be associated publicly or, if I can help it, privately with tobacco, alcohol, or pharmaceuticals, an option that fame and wealth have afforded me. In the time frame that concerns us in this chapter I would gladly have belched on microphone or camera for half an hour if the money was right. Or even if it wasn't right. My first major sponsor, the Roma Wine Company, illustrates early compromises that had to be made.

Dad Linkletter, who followed my career with interest if not always with understanding, preached loud and long about the evils of drink and was quite shocked when he first heard me publicly extolling the virtues of the fermented grape. I knew that would happen, but I simply couldn't afford then to put principle ahead of practicality; that is a luxury reserved for those who have made it or for those who never do.

Well, Dad Linkletter wanted the best for me. After ascertaining that I did not personally indulge (the rare times I have had more than one drink my metabolism has given my convictions a big assist) he set out to find justification in his Bible for my erring ways. Ecclesiastes 9:7 came to my rescue: "Go thy way, eat thy bread with joy, and drink thy wine with a merry heart; for God now accepteth thy works." While I doubt that He meant the Roma Wine Company, that and similar references pacified my dad and made it somewhat easier to go my way.

My career was well and truly launched in San Francisco and my voice was heard regularly for the first time outside the U.S. and Canada. I had a morning program called "Date at Eight," sponsored by Tru Pak Foods, on which I read for fifteen minutes a *Reader's Digest*-style roundup of interesting trivia put together by a writer that I hired. The program caught the attention of the director of short-wave transmission for the federal government and he asked me, as a service to the United States, to repeat an expanded version of the show, which would be beamed daily to a number of foreign countries.

Once again that strange happenstance, that guiding hand that some people call fate, reached out and touched me. I was never, even back then, one for offering my services gratis; and surely, I reasoned, the world's greatest sponsor, the U.S. government, was well able to pay my modest fee. But this was 1940. World War II had begun abroad and our sympathies as a nation were becoming firmly established, so I did the patriotic thing and began my global broadcasts. For me it was a stiff test of patriotism, because I not only read the stuff for nothing but had to pay out of my own pocket the writer who assembled it.

Looking back, I suppose it was a natural decision to make. But as it turned out (was unseen guidance involved?), taking on that freebie saved my career, and perhaps my life, in a way that I could not then have foreseen.

Chapter Eleven

When the Japanese attacked Pearl Harbor on December 7, 1941, I had already been involved in the war effort for more than a year.

In those days the word *propaganda* represented something strange and somehow not quite suited to the openness with which Americans conducted their national and international affairs. However, to those of us in the business of communicating the written and spoken word, the effective use of propaganda had already proven to be a deadly instrument in the wrong hands, second only to armed force in its destructive ability. Indeed, in many ways propaganda, though not a direct killer, was even more dangerous than confronting armies because it created a climate of aggression and hate without which those armies would have little reason to exist.

In 1941 the general public only dimly understood, or cared, how Joseph Goebbels, Nazi "minister of popular enlightenment," had refined mass indoctrination techniques to a degree unknown to that time. The clubfooted Heidelberg graduate had been largely responsible for selling the Nazi philosophy to the German nation. His techniques roused the citizens to such a pitch that they felt compelled to commit their sons and daughters and themselves to the cause of Aryan supremacy.

The British and the Russians understood the impact that Goebbels' half-truths and distortions, endlessly repeated over powerful short-wave transmitters, were having on world opinion. Each country had its own international service that presented news in foreign languages as well as in English; but the United States, because of its great ocean "moats" and a general inclination to leave other countries alone, was way behind in this important field.

"Date at Eight" had begun as a newsy local morning program but by mid-1941 was being heard globally, helping to establish an American presence in areas that were hearing other nations' versions of world events. Although I did not engage in incendiary propaganda, I did reflect our government's growing sympathy for Great Britain and the pitifully few Allies by reporting events factually. The more people around the world who knew, for example, that we had turned over fifty destroyers to Britain under a lend-lease arrangement, or that in August 1941 Roosevelt and Churchill had met on a warship on the high seas to formulate the Atlantic Charter as a general statement of democratic aims, the better it was for the embattled Allied powers. The mere knowledge that the world's biggest industrial power was sympathetic to Britain's cause did a great deal to counteract the image of invincibility that Goebbels was trying to project.

When I received my 1-A draft classification with orders to report to the local draft board, I felt that I was already part of the war effort and my State Department superiors more than agreed. They notified the board that I was a vital part of their program, and the board was very empathetic when I appeared before it. One member, a kindly looking white-haired gentleman wearing horn-rimmed glasses, leaned forward.

"What," he asked, "is your salary, Mr. Linkletter?"

"My salary?"

"Yes. What does the government pay you to do these broadcasts?"

"Oh," I smiled broadly. "Nothing. I don't take a cent for it. It's all free."

"I see," he replied in a not so kindly tone. "Volunteer work."

"Well, not exactly," I explained. "I was asked to do it as a favor to the government."

"People volunteer all the time to get out of joining the army, Mr. Linkletter," said the nasty old hoary-haired gentleman. "If you're not being paid, you can't be deferred."

He told me to report the next afternoon for processing and induction.

Well, our house wasn't exactly a fun place that night. I was prepared to do whatever was expected of me, of course, but I knew how important the radio transmissions were. The irony of being unable to continue them because I had been trying to do something patriotic was not lost on me. I felt that I would be far more useful in front of a microphone than peeling potatoes. Too, I would be less than candid if I didn't say that I wasn't exactly looking forward to being shot at, but hundreds of thousands of other fellows were in the same boat, so Lois and I tried to adjust ourselves to my impending career change.

Next morning in the mailbox was a legal-size envelope with a government frank from Nelson Rockefeller's Committee on Interamerican Affairs, the group that ran our overseas transmissions. The committee, I read, had foreseen that its key people, many of whom, like myself, were public-spirited performers working for nothing, would be drafted, so it was putting me on salary and giving me a firm contract to expand my broadcasts in keeping with the new war condition.

The contract represented an automatic deferment and I was

soon more heavily involved in the war effort. Meantime, I had my commercial commitments, with their rewards and hazards. When Treasure Island closed I moved a show I had started there, "What Do You Think?" into the Telenews Theater of Market Street where it was sponsored by the Albert S. Samuels Company, a jewelry firm. I would choose a controversial question, as easy then as now, and have members of the audience debate the pros and cons.

One day on the show I asked for anyone's opinion of the daily press. A man stood up and for two or three minutes blistered the *San Francisco Examiner* in particular and the Hearst press in general, including some rather pointed criticisms of William Randolph Hearst himself. When he sat down I asked for opposing views. Silence. I asked again. Still silence. Not one person would defend Mr. Hearst or his papers. I sensed immediately that this was bad news for me and signed off, promising to bring up the topic again in the next broadcast so that we could hear the other side of the story.

I cleared up a few technical details with my sound engineer and was about to leave the theater lobby when an usher called me to the phone. A performer likes to know that people are listening or watching out there, and if the home audience happens to include prominent people that's icing on the cake. Usually.

It was never really clear to me whether William Randolph Hearst personally was listening to the broadcast high atop his mountain at San Simeon or whether one of his minions in the city had phoned him. Either way the voice of the Hearst editor on the phone left little doubt that the famous publisher was absolutely convinced that I had loaded that theater audience against him. He had issued an edict that neither the name Art Linkletter nor any of his programs ever again be mentioned in any Hearst paper. His paper even removed my shows from the radio listings; I was anonymously producing something called "To Be Announced" roughly twenty-five times per week as far as Hearst was concerned. Talk about saturation programming, that show must really have been a winner.

But my sponsors and I were the losers. The radio listings were extremely important and I had to live in Hearst-imposed isolation while trying to make a buck. It was not until nearly two years later, when I was coming on strong in Hollywood, that I was restored to favor. At that time Louella Parsons, at the height of her power, befriended me and interceded with Mr. Hearst in my behalf. My return to grace was especially important because I was beginning to go network and the Hearst papers, then as now, covered the nation's most populous areas.

While in San Francisco I was given an opportunity to contribute greatly to American preparedness in a much more direct and more satisfying manner than my short-wave broadcasts. Norrie Nash, a friend of mine who was public-relations director for the Kaiser shipyards, called and offered me a most challenging assignment. Kaiser was just beginning to build the now famous Liberty ships, which would transport men and matériel around the globe. There were five major shipyards in the Bay Area that would eventually turn out one Liberty ship per day, an extraordinary achievement.

The shipyards, Nash told me, were in danger of not being able to live up to their potential to supply the sorely needed transport for the Allied powers. Manpower was rapidly being siphoned off by the armed services; the draft boards did not feel that building merchant ships had the same priority as building up an army, navy, and air force. It was, of course, a somewhat shortsighted policy, but everyone was trying to do his best in those early war years and priorities were not always clear.

Henry Kaiser had hit upon the then unheard-of idea of having women help build the ships. Housewives as welders seemed an unlikely possibility. The song "Rosie the Riveter" may be a museum piece now, but it mirrored a radical change in the woman's place in the scheme of things. In a patriotic, practical form of women's lib, wives, daughters, and even grandmothers drastically altered their lifestyles. Instead of shouting largely meaningless slogans and calling press conferences, American women learned to handle acetylene torches and power hammers, and helped create modern industrial miracles.

How to woo women from traditional roles as mothers or waitresses or office workers or teachers to demanding shipyard work? (I've often wondered why so many present-day female proponents of equal rights want to be bestselling authors or presidents of advertising agencies rather than coal miners or sanitation workers. Could be the low visibility of the latter two occupations.) Norrie Nash felt that because of my popularity and the type of shows I put on the air, women would identify with my suggestions on this matter.

As radio director of the Kaiser shipyards I would go on the air to acquaint women with the desperate national need, assure them that special nurseries would give their children proper care, and tell them about the very good working conditions as well as the excellent pay. I would also plan noontime entertainment on the company's internal radio "network," organize broadcasts of ship launchings, and generally act as the voice of Kaiser shipyards.

I took the job and we soon had a highly efficient training and entertainment program going. Women became convinced that there was nothing unfeminine in donning overalls and making, in many cases, more money than their husbands in behalf of the war effort. That job, plus my short-wave broadcasts as well as all my regular commercial shows, really kept me hopping and forced me to establish some work and play habits that I practice to this day.

Quite simply, I had to organize my life in order to survive. I was doing so many things that I soon found it necessary each evening to type for myself a list of activities for the next day, and once each week to type a list of next week's activities. After I moved to Hollywood, the demands of two network shows, an unending string of personal appearances, and, as time went on, larger and larger business commitments added a three-month time projection to my daily and weekly schedule, as well as a third list comprising current business activities that required my attention. I carry the updated list with me and refer to it constantly, sometimes to the amusement of friends and business associates.

Clyde Vandeburg tells a story about a trip he and I took to inspect Linkletter's Place, a large cattle and sheep ranch I own in the southern part of Western Australia, near the Indian Ocean port of Esperance. That was no small trip in the days of piston-engine planes, when we seemed to refuel on every atoll between Hawaii and Sydney. Aside from the expense involved, I had to clear otherwise productive time in order to make the journey. Once there, I would face decisions regarding livestock acquisitions and sales, ground clearing, and planting that would involve in the long run hundreds of thousands of dollars. So it was no simple vacation jaunt we were taking.

As Clyde recalls it, our four-engine plane was somewhere over the South Pacific when I pulled out my wallet, extracted my typed weekly schedule and consulted the section under "Deals"—business matters that I wanted to keep on top of. I turned to Clyde and, quite offhandedly, remarked: "Remind me to send Lee [Lee Ray, my private secretary] a memo from Sydney about a stock dividend due today."

"Can't it wait?" he asked.

"Well, it's due today. I want her to check on it."

"How much is it?"

I consulted my sheet. "Forty-seven dollars and eighty cents," I replied. Then, I'm told, having completed that transaction, I closed my eyes and fell asleep.

My love affair with Australia began back in 1954 when Allen Chase, an investor and banker, Charles Correll, the Andy of "Amos 'n' Andy," Bob Cummings, and I formed a syndicate that we promptly dubbed the Hollywood Pioneers. Our purpose was to investigate the possibilities of growing rice in Australia's Northern Territory.

Now that last sentence is probably the most oversimplified, naive statement you will read in this entire book. It's like calling World War II a police action.

Australia's Top End, the extreme tip of the Northern Territory jutting out into the Timor and Arafura seas, represented a vast, largely undeveloped frontier that, as far as we were concerned, had three things going for it. The government was willing to make available to our group 500,000 acres at a very good price, free, provided we agreed to finance the clearing, irrigation, planting, and general development of the area. The property, near a place called Humpty Doo, lay on either side of the Adelaide River, which teemed with crocodiles capable of knocking a full-size cow into the water and crushing it like a bovine canapé.

Although the river's inhabitants might have tipped us off that all was not what it seemed at the Top End, the Hollywood Pioneers expected some frontier hazards. We remained wary of, but undeterred by, the crocs. It was the second feature of this vast, untapped natural resource that really appealed to us: we could grow rice there. Test earth bores produced samples of alluvial soil to a depth of eighty-five feet, very rich seedbed, indeed. Frost-free nights and intensely hot days provided a climate ideal for rice growing.

Chinese laborers, imported to Darwin to help build a railroad in years past, occasionally spilled some of their rice rations along the right-of-way where, we were reliably informed, it took root and grew wild, unaided by human hand. The Australian government, anxious to open up a new source of international exchange, hired experts from places like Thailand and Cambodia to advise. They proclaimed Humpty Doo a ricey Canaan and asked when they could place orders for the first crop. That, of course, was the third item of interest in our investment trinity: a market for our product. The whole Southeast Asian fan from India to Japan eats rice, often more than the smaller nations can produce. Not only would we supply that much needed staple, but we would also turn a nice profit for our investment, twin circumstances that were not lost on investors back home who now wanted in.

Despite the land grant, the investment was substantial. Ground had to be cleared, and drainage ditches and dikes constructed to handle the monsoon season—referred to by Aussies, with characteristic understatement, as The Wet—before planting could begin. That meant importing men, heavy equipment, and supplies from the south by rail, ship, and, to a lesser extent, air. Yet our excitement mounted when we saw the sturdy, lush strain of Thai rice that we selected begin to yield an excellent crop.

Unfortunately, we had not reckoned with the annual migration of the magpie goose. As his name suggests, the magpie is a rather attractive fowl, whose mottled black and white plumage is not unlike that of our own American magpie. The goose also possesses a voracious appetite and an indefatigable kamikaze spirit. Once an objective has been sighted, say, our beautiful rice fields, nothing but death will deter the goose from eating its fill.

The magpie geese came first in hundreds, then thousands, then tens of thousands in their annual quest for the tender green shoots that grow wild on the Top End. They found, to their boundless joy, that someone had planted seemingly endless fields of a gourmet dish, long-grain rice from Thailand. Like a plague of goose-size locusts, they ate everything in sight. In areas that were just being seeded, the sturdy magpie would follow along behind our hand seeders and gobble up the expensive imported hors d'oeuvres almost before they touched the ground. We tried seeding several hundred acres by air, but the magpies, delighted at our thoughtfulness, flew happily along below our planes vacuuming up the airborne seeds.

I am not a hunter and would never use a gun to kill an innocent wild animal, but all bets were off with the magpies. The Australian government declared open season on the ravenous geese, but that didn't seem to help. There were too many of them and they refused to be intimidated. We strung miles of shiny metal cans, set up scarecrows, and let off ear-splitting carbon guns, but the magpies, perhaps because of their oriental background, *loved* the noise and glitter—every day was New Year's Day to those stuffed geese.

When the magpies, finally sated, took off for parts unknown, we found that some of our crop had survived, enough at least to show potential customers what we had while we planned a magpie defense. We had evaluated our damage and were about to order the surviving rice harvested when the annual monsoon hit. We, of course, had been building dikes and dredging canals in anticipation of the sixty-five-inch annual rainfall. We were prepared to drain off heavy rains over the three-month season. What we should have known, in an area where crocodiles inhabit the river and magpies screech joyously at the sound of gunfire, was that much of that rainfall descended all at once.

I have never seen rain like that, before or since. In March 1956 we measured fifteen inches of rain in a two-day deluge that washed out our remaining rice. It was enough to send yours truly on a walkabout, the Australian aborigine's habit of periodically abandoning civilization and living by himself in the bush. But anyone who has produced television shows in Hollywood is not going to be shaken up by mere natural disasters. The Hollywood Pioneers, enthused by the quality of our rice and the market availability, agreed to try again.

We brought in larger, most sophisticated pumps, built bigger dikes, dug deeper channels. We installed a complicated sequential firing system that would enable our batteries of carbon guns to blast away every three minutes, giving the magpie geese no rest. And then we planted our second crop—but at the beginning of a season that would receive an all-time record rainfall for Australia. Thousands of acres were converted into a vast quagmire in which even the sturdy Thai rice could not survive.

We had one consolation. The magpies didn't get any rice either. Our equipment losses mounted. Pumps, working frantically to drain away the water, either blew up or burned out. Dikes collapsed, burying other heavy machinery and causing our levee roads to be hopelessly blocked by mired tractors, trucks, and jeeps.

Yet we were not prepared to concede defeat. That heavy rain was, after all, a once-in-a-lifetime Wet and some of our seedlings had survived. So we cultivated what was left, certain that next year, with a reasonable rainfall, the right preparation, and our antimagpie forces in action, we would begin to produce premium rice.

The rain was kind to us for this our third try, but we had failed to allow for the water buffalo that roam the Top End in herds of thousands, reminiscent of our own western buffalo two centuries ago. Water buffalo love greens and can smell tasty growth from miles downwind. The herds descended on Humpty Doo and what they didn't eat, they trampled. As if that were not enough, when the normal water build-up receded we were introduced to a season that the Australians euphemistically call The Dry.

The Australian Dry makes Death Valley in June seem like the garden spot of California. Daytime temperatures soar to a hundred twenty degrees and drop to ninety at night. The Adelaide River is reduced to a trickle, forcing the crocs and the buffalo inland. Almost overnight the rich soil turns into a cracked, parched flat which extends forty miles inland and on which nothing can grow. The Hollywood Pioneers, two million dollars poorer, called it a day.

But Australia, magpie geese, buffalo, Wet, Dry, and all had gotten into my blood. I liked the people. Strong, iconoclastic, given to view the world with a wry wit, they seemed to me very much like our own 1800s settlers, eager to challenge and tame undeveloped land. I had heard that there was interesting land available a continent away from Humpty Doo, at Esperance, on the southern coast of Western Australia and washed by the Indian Ocean. It was interesting in that it was uncultivated, unpopulated, and covered with low brush and scrub suitable, at that time, for nothing. But Esperance, once a bustling ocean port during the 1891 gold rush at Coolgardie a few miles north, had a fine harbor. A private survey I commissioned concluded that with proper irrigation and some supplemental feeding the land could easily support three and perhaps four sheep per acre, a very good ratio.

In short, Esperance had all the classic Linkletter investment ingredients: good basic potential, more than a little risk, and eventually a profitable operation. It offered one more lure—a pioneer challenge. That I might be instrumental in opening up a whole new area for exploration, settlement, and commerce, an opportunity presented to very few men in this age of dwindling frontiers, appealed to my own pioneer instinct.

The irrepressible Allen Chase had put together a syndicate that hoped eventually to sell 1.5 million acres of land north of Esperance in 2,000-acre parcels, but all that he had then was the hope. Australians and Englishmen had tried working the area but were forced to give up because of a combination of factors similar to those we encountered at Humpty Doo. The Esperance Plains Company, Allen's outfit, owned nothing but potential until someone went in there and actually proved that the land could be put to gainful use.

The challenge was there, and looking back, I think that I was smarting a little at the Humpty Doo failure because I had not had enough say in what was going on. The people involved at Top End did their best but I have always felt more comfortable winning or losing on my own merits rather than relying on anyone else. So I bought 22,000 acres at fifty-five cents an acre, a modest investment except when viewed in the context of my recent heavy loss in the same country and under circumstances not unlike those I now faced.

I shall never forget, after a bumpy sixty-mile, three-hour jeep

ride up from Esperance, standing beside Lois on a knoll overlooking our property, which seemed to consist of horizon to
horizon scrub brush. I said nothing to her but I must now confess
that I wondered for the briefest moment what I was doing there.
Some stubbornness perhaps, a refusal to be beaten by that
sprawling, fascinating down-under land. But something else too,
something I've described before in other situations—a feeling
that I was destined to be there, that somehow my experience
at Top End had been but a testing ground and that now I was
deemed ready to meet and overcome this primary challenge by
utilizing my own wits and resources.

Aware of most of the pitfalls involved in Australian ranching
and also acutely conscious of the fact that I could be on the scene
only for brief, widely scattered periods, I hired a young farmer
named John Hagon, a man risen from the soil who combined
a practical knowledge of and love for the land with a highly
disciplined, informed mind. Today John Hagon not only man-
ages the 22,000-acre Linkletter Place at Esperance but also
works his own station, as ranches are called there.

In the beginning the going was slow, rough, and expensive.
We first built shelter for ourselves, then cleared and irrigated
land for the livestock, and erected fences to control their movement. We had to bulldoze and grade our own roads as well as
build our own bridges and culverts. Everything—lumber, nails,
cement, gasoline, oil, medicine, and the many other standard
items that most of us take for granted—had to be trucked from
Esperance.

Eventually Linkletter's Place began to take shape. There were
outbuildings, workshops, and living quarters for the increasing
number of jackaroos and drovers (sheepmen and cowboys) we
were hiring. And with the addition of Angus and Hereford cattle
and Merino sheep, we became aware that our growing spread
also needed its own school. Thus we began what amounted to
a two-year agricultural college. Using films supplied by the Australian Agricultural Department, John trained and "graduated"

four jackaroos a year, some of whom stayed with us. Others went out to start ranches of their own.

Today that original 22,000 acres is valued conservatively at over three million dollars. On a recent trip I took a jeep ride to the top of Condingup Mountain, overlooking our spread, and thought back to Lois's and my first glimpse of a barren, inhospitable sea of scrub. Seeing now the homes, paddocks, worksheds, and neat fences crisscrossing a sea of green pasture; and knowing that over forty thousand head of sheep and some one thousand head of cattle were roaming our 22,000 acres, I felt a tremendous sense of accomplishment. I would be falsely modest if I did not say that, atop that mountain, my excitement was greater and of a different kind than I have ever experienced in all my eventful life.

I had accepted a challenge and won. Well, I have done that before, many times. Here, however, I could justly claim to be partly responsible for the opening up of a miniempire in an area where no man built before. More than one million acres are presently being developed in the Esperance area, and wheat growing and sheep and cattle raising abound. A vibrancy is about the place, as well as a sense of accomplishment, which feeds back to me in a special sort of way.

Our original one rutty dirt lane has blossomed into more than five hundred access roads. And Esperance harbor, now boasting a bulk-grain terminal and a slaughtering plant, has been dredged to a depth of thirty-two feet and a new berth serves the increasing oceangoing traffic. The coastal districts of South Australia and Western Australia are fast becoming that country's richest agricultural areas, and I believe the sheep yield, with proper cropping and management, can rise to six, perhaps eight, per acre. My confidence has led me, with some other investors, to buy 970,000 acres at Anna Plains on the western coast. The property has an eighty-mile beach front, ideal for getting away from it all.

But it all had to start somewhere. And to this day I feel a special sense of accomplishment that I believe is the privilege of few men today. If destiny indeed took me to Esperance, it surely also had a hand in a personal request, regarding Australia, from the President of the United States, a request that could have altered my entire career.

Chapter Twelve

Personal relationships with U.S. Presidents and sprawling ranches in far-off Australia were the stuff of dreams to the young San Francisco radio personality walking briskly up Powell Street on his way to line up people for "Who's Dancing Tonight" in the St. Francis Hotel. My new Kaiser duties, my short-wave transmissions, and my regular shows tended to submerge me in thought, and I was not entirely conscious of my surroundings as I neared the graceful building facing Union Square.

I passed several sidewalk newsstands before I registered what surely must have been the most spectacular double take in history. On that day, December 8, 1942, exactly one year after the United States had declared war on Japan, I had my own crisis. The newspaper headlines announced in large boldface type, ART LINKLETTER INDICTED.

My first thought was that it was some sort of a gag set up by a rival station to break through my on-the-air display of cool. But the thought came and went in the time it took me to grab a paper—I don't even recall whether I paid for it or not—and duck into the nearest office-building lobby. Yes, I actually did that. I read the details of the lead story with a sinking heart. I had been indicted by a federal grand jury for lying about my birthplace, falsely claiming to be an American citizen, illegally voting in an election, and stating that I had never been out of the United States.

I stood staring, unseeing, at the rest of the front page and experienced real panic for the first time since that tramp pulled back the hammer of his revolver in the boxcar on a siding in Walla Walla, Washington. If convicted, I finally read on, I could be sentenced to five years in prison and fined five thousand dollars.

To understand how I felt, as I numbly dialed the office of attorney William A. "Bill" O'Brien from the lobby pay phone, you must appreciate the public mood at that crucial period in our nation's history. The distinction between "alien" and "enemy alien" was virtually nonexistent in the mind of the general public. And I was a very special case. I had represented myself as a Mr. War Effort, a true-blue American to hundreds of thousands of people.

It was an accurate representation in my mind, but I feared that wouldn't matter once the press got through with me. Even worse, I was engaged in sensitive war-related work for Kaiser. Suddenly the short-wave transmissions, of which I was especially proud, hung like an albatross around my neck, reminding me that this indicted alien would be accused of broadcasting who knows what secrets to America's enemies.

As I sat in Bill O'Brien's office I was about as low as I've ever been in my life. I had chosen to assume that mother and father Linkletter had become naturalized Americans, making me automatically a citizen. It was a self-deception made the more easy because I felt like an American. Who would have thought that a grand jury would have found anything sinister in the fact that I was born in Moose Jaw? Presumably I had spent the first six months of my life there cleverly setting up an international spy network that would bear fruit in San Francisco thirty years later.

Even in my distress I was not bitter because I never have believed in complaining about or explaining a misfortune. Years later Jack Tyler, a friend with whom I have been involved in some big but not always successful business transactions, told an associate—who was kind enough to pass it along to me—"You'll get no gripes from Art, no matter how the deal goes." I can think of worse sentiments for one's epitaph.

In San Francisco I saw my career, to say nothing of my personal liberty, in jeopardy as I answered my attorney's searching questions. Yes, for convenience I had given my birthplace as Lowell, Massachusetts, on my security clearance application for my short-wave work. Yes, I voted in an election. Yes, I had forgotten that Denver Colorado Fox and I had been in South America. Yes, I had applied for my naturalization papers and stated that I had never been out of the country.

Naturalization papers? My conscience is what did me in. As I became more involved in the war effort I began increasingly to feel uneasy about my not being a citizen. If I had let the whole thing pass, chances are I would be writing this without having to report the trauma of those weeks of uncertainty in San Francisco. Even though I knew nothing else in my conscious lifetime except feeling, thinking, and behaving like an American, I understood deep down that I was not, and the constant living of even so innocent a lie finally drove me to set it all right. In September 1942 I went to the naturalization bureau of the U.S. Immigration Service and applied for American citizenship. And that is when it all started to hit the fan.

Bill O'Brien, as lawyers will, gave me the heartening news that there had been four very recent cases similar to mine and that each had pleaded guilty and been sentenced to a year in jail.

"I don't think," he said, reaching for the phone to call the U.S. marshal, "we better go the guilty route. We'll plead *nolo contendere.*"

"What's that?" I asked.

"You don't admit guilt but the implication is that you don't have a defense."

"Okay."

I felt my world crashing down as we drove to the marshal's office to surrender. My name meant everything to me. I was only now getting a jump on the career for which I had worked so hard. Now Lois and I faced not only professional oblivion but personal ostracism. I have since learned the truth of the cliché that things often seem worse than they are, but anyone would have had a hard time selling me on that while I was being booked, fingerprinted, and photographed by a deputy marshal.

We posted bail and were set for a court appearance before federal judge Michael J. Roche. O'Brien asked that I be given probation.

"Perhaps," Judge Roche addressed me, "your success has made you feel that it is not necessary to obey the law."

"I never had any such thought, Your Honor."

"If I were to excuse you it would set a precedent."

I stood there, anything but the self-assured, glib performer, waiting for him to continue.

"It is not a case for probation. Probation denied."

For once no ad-lib, no fast reply that would turn the situation to my advantage, no easy smile that lets everyone know that everything is under control. Because everything was not under control. The judge's next words came through a maze of numbed senses.

"I fine you five hundred dollars or six months in jail," he said. "I am, with this sentence, extending you the charity of this country."

Then, while I was still trying to pull myself together, he explained that my motives were sound; he felt I would make a good citizen and he had denied probation because a probationary period would have delayed my citizenship. It was a memorable morning in my life; I learned citizenship should never be taken for granted and that so long as there are men like Judge Roche in this country, able to apply the laws with compassion, our survival as a nation is assured.

The grand jury is something else again. In many instances I feel it wields too much power. No reasonable person reviewing my case could have concluded that there was criminal intent, yet the secrecy of the grand-jury system not only denied me a hearing but condemned me publicly in a most cavalier fashion. The grand jury serves a useful watchdog purpose, but I often wonder whether it, like so many other investigative and quasi-judicial institutions, has assumed an identity never intended when it was first constituted.

In my case the grand-jury investigators had learned that my real name was Arthur Gordon Kelly, born in Moose Jaw, Saskatchewan, Canada, of an unwed mother and a father who allegedly lived in the nearby city of Regina. All that didn't bother me. In subsequent years on radio and television I made no secret of the fact that I was an orphan because I felt that it might help other kids who started out the same way.

What did continue to disturb me was the authenticity of the grand-jury information. Somehow, I can't hope to explain why, I never really felt like Arthur Gordon Kelly. If I had another name, another identity, it was yet to be discovered. That extra sense, the feeling of something removed from my physical presence that I've spoken of before, continued to badger me whenever a reporter or someone else would ask me if I had ever located my biological mother and father. I would pass off the question by saying that I was happy with my present name and that it wouldn't be fair to everyone concerned for me suddenly to descend on a mother, probably with her own family, who had once disowned me and announce my true identity.

I have always made a personal distinction between the reproductive and bringing-up phases of parenthood. Producing a baby does not automatically qualify anyone for the title of parent, meaning someone who accepts the responsibility of loving and raising a child. I always remember the story of the little kid who, when told "God made you," replied, "Well, I'm not finished yet."

The nagging feeling of unfinished business regarding my identity came to a head when I decided to write this book. I knew with a sudden sense of finality that I had to set the record straight, for my own satisfaction and because I intended honestly to discuss my emotions and experiences.

Meanwhile, once again, a kind providence intervened and pointed the way for me. I was invited to appear at the Regina Provincial Fair. With Irv Atkins, an associate who often travels with me on personal appearances, off I went and performed before a warm and appreciative audience.

For once my public business was only a secondary part of my trip. Much was made of my having been born in nearby Moose Jaw and of my real name being Kelly, so when I visited my birthplace for the first time since I was six months old, what appeared to be the whole town turned out to bid me welcome.

Fascinating things began happening as soon as I had been ceremoniously "arrested" by the chief of police, taken to the town lockup as an impostor, and then, with great fanfare and the clicking of cameras, released by a mayoral pardon. First, I discovered that, as a six-month-old, I had made an astonishing number of friends. Several people remembered the Kelly baby as the cutest thing they had ever seen. Not only that, but I was an amazingly precocious child. At a chamber of commerce luncheon in my honor a man came up to me and the conversation, to the best of my recollection, began something like this.

"Hey, Art, remember the time you and I skipped school and were crossing Mrs. Mahoney's back pasture?"

I have perfected a noncommittal smile for such occasions, and that I laid on this gentleman while considering my options. I could tell him that the incident couldn't possibly have happened, thereby offending and embarrassing him in front of his friends. That would have been cruel; anyhow, I felt he believed what he was saying. People can talk themselves into almost any relationship where a show-business personality is concerned. My alternative was to go along with his harmless story. Even though I knew better, I fell into the classic trap of verifying his recollection rather than taking some deft evasive action.

"Gosh," I said, "those were great days, weren't they?"

"Remember that old horse she had tethered out back?"

"How could I forget it?"

"And what you did with that horse?" My imaginary school chum, seeing that he and I now were the center of attention, began to relish his newly acquired status.

My private warning bell rang but I knew that I was in too deep. "Well," I said in what I hoped was a conspiratorial tone, "maybe we just better forget that one."

"Oh, no you don't, Art," my old buddy clapped me good-naturedly on the arm. "You've got to tell 'em about it."

"I think it would be better coming from you."

"*Me* tell a story better than Art Linkletter?" He looked around, acknowledging everyone's laughter. "Come on, now."

"Why that's the whole idea," I told him. "Coming from me it might sound as though I were making some of it up, but you were there and it's really your story about me."

The notion that he could tell a story about me appealed to him and he went into a long narrative about how I had climbed onto a fence, jumped on the horse's back, and was riding it all over the pasture when Mrs. Mahoney came out and chased us both over the fence with her broom; all of it, of course, totally without foundation in fact.

The point is that well-meaning, honest people do this frequently with prominent personalities and we all have learned to guard against being trapped. Although most of those situations, like my Moose Jaw friend's story, are conceived in all innocence, some are not. People who want to draw attention to themselves or create a relationship that can lead to their financial gain through exploitation or, in rare cases, extortion, will attempt to catch their target off guard and steer a conversation in a certain direction. If your favorite movie or television star seems a trifle abrupt in person, it may be because he or she has been burned once too often and feels that being cooperative is simply not worth the risk.

After the luncheon Irv Atkins and I went to the local courthouse, searched through some dusty records, and finally learned that mine had been transferred to Regina some time ago. We then went to the local *Times-Herald* office, checked its files back to July 17, 1912, but found no mention in the births column. Then I realized that a small-town paper probably would not have the staff to enable it to report births and deaths on the day after they occurred, so I looked at the next day and the next after that. Sure enough, there it was, Effie Brown had given birth to a son three days before and it listed the address.

A quick check of the street directory showed no such address existed, but one of the *Times-Herald* staff recalled that back in 1912 or '13 a town planning council had changed a lot of the street names to avoid having one street designated three or four different ways as it crossed town. At the local library a very kind reference librarian checked back and found the original and present names of that particular street.

We drove to the address listed in the paper, a very modest white frame house that looked as though it had been given tender loving care since at least 1912. I knocked on the door. An attractive young lady in her early thirties answered.

"Do you mind if I come in?" I asked. "I'm Art Linkletter and I was born here."

She stood staring at me in disbelief, then half turned and called over her shoulder, "Honey, come here. It's," and she looked back at me again, "it's Art Linkletter. Really."

Well, Irv and I made their day and they, ours. After tea and cookies the husband took us on a conducted tour, showing how the place had been remodeled inside. We drove to the site of the orphanage where Effie Brown had deposited me before she returned to Regina. Though greatly expanded, it was still there, the only difference being that it was now an old folks' home that, I must admit, I had no desire to enter.

Back in Regina we went to the provincial archives. After some diligent searching we found my birth certificate, from which my father's name had been erased, obviously to avoid the scandal of siring me out of wedlock. However, by holding the aging document up to the light I could see enough of the original writing to learn, for the first time in all these years, that my name was in fact not Kelly. I cannot say for certain, but to the best of my ability to make out erased and faded handwriting my father's name was Kalle or something very similar. Etymologically it might well be an anglicization of the Scottish Kail, and that would move me across the North Channel to Scotland and provide some justification for my daughter Sharon's earlier reference to inherited thrift.

Had that grand jury in San Francisco been less persistent in its investigation of my background, I probably would be writing this without ever having seen documented proof of my birth. The fact that I have seen it should be reassuring in this identity-conscious age, but somehow that proof does not quite compensate me for my trying days and weeks between the indictment and the fine. Although I do not question the motives of those grand jurors, they did have a ripe candidate in a young, barely established performer with a growing family who was somewhat cowed by the monolithic power of big government.

Since those early days I have had occasion to be singled out by public servants seeking to badger me and they have found to their dismay that I am now not easily intimidated. The most widely publicized and misreported instance of my jousting with some well-meaning, as well as certain cretinous, guardians of the public weal involves what Sir Arthur Conan Doyle might have titled *The Curious Affair of National Liberty Insurance.*

National Liberty is a direct-response company that provides supplemental hospital coverage. Instead of dealing through agents the company reaches potential clients by extensive use of advertising in all media and conducts business directly with the policyholder. Put simply, it means that National Liberty, unlike most insurance companies, spends money through mail-order, newspaper, magazine, radio, and television advertising before signing up a client rather than through long-term commission payments to agents after the policy is acquired. This method of operation, the company believes, saves money for all concerned while efficiently providing needed supplemental coverage.

When I was asked by Arthur DeMoss, the company president, and Bill Shipley, vice president and marketing manager, to become the official spokesman for National Liberty and serve on the board of directors, the first thing I did was to have them investigated, with their knowledge and consent. I liked the idea of being a board member rather than merely a highly paid face and voice because, as I've said before, I like to participate actively in new, for me, commercial ventures. So I was especially careful to satisfy myself that the company was sound, was offering a legitimate service, and, most important, was following through with loss payments.

I asked to visit their headquarters at Valley Forge, Pennsylvania, and was absolutely astonished at what I found there. Not only was there a bustling, positive atmosphere about the place, but, unique to my business experience, a Christian, God-fearing attitude prevailed to the extent that no meeting, whether a board meeting or an employees' training session, ever opened or closed without prayer. I learned too that Arthur DeMoss spent a great deal of money sponsoring Christian businessmen's seminars and charitable organizations.

DeMoss and Shipley wanted me to take an active part on their team by becoming a marketing consultant and a board member, in addition to being their public spokesman. That suited me just fine. Frankly, so did the remuneration. In addition to receiving a very sizable yearly retainer I was given a substantial stock option, which appeals to me much more than cash at this point in my career.

In 1971 National Liberty initiated a multi-million-dollar advertising campaign built around me; it is a matter of record that the increase in company business was believed to be one of the greatest responses to a multimedia campaign in the history of American direct-response advertising. The people to whom I appealed, the average working or retired person who either did not have enough premium money to attract a conventional agent or needed that little extra coverage to take care of expenses above those paid for by public or private group plans, reacted so strongly that my television commercials, showing in all fifty states, themselves became topics of conversation.

Then, when our growth was outstripping most established insurance companies across the country, curious things began happening. The opening shot was fired by a Herbert Dennenberg of the Pennsylvania State Insurance Department, who asserted, among other things, that "Art Linkletter's advertising is Madison Avenue hogwash, and it should be discounted ninety percent. The public should be told that he receives $50,000 per year in compensation."

Dennenberg, who had political ambitions (he later ran for the U.S. Senate and the good people of Pennsylvania in their wisdom selected someone else), made other charges—the company was making too much money; it was not paying out enough in losses; and its policy contained a preexisting-illness clause, which designated a waiting period before certain illnesses present at the time of the signing of the policy would be covered, and which "is one of the most troublesome provisions in the health-insurance business."

Dennenberg's allegations were simply that, allegations. The

company effectively answered all charges point by point, and made germane information available to any prospective policy-holder, as it does today. At no time was there anything remotely resembling civil or criminal proceedings against the company in Pennsylvania or in any other state. It was only after I had over three hundred million exposures in magazine ads, on radio, and television, that anyone chose to climb onto the publicity bandwagon and question our success.

Officials of other states, seeing Dennenberg suddenly cata-pulted into national prominence, began examining my com-mercials word by word. In many cases they issued press releases trumpeting consumer protection (Ralph Nader was hot in those days) without bothering even to inform the company of its sup-posed transgressions. The company, licensed in every state in which it does business, frequently changed the wording at the whim of an insurance commissioner even though there was not the remotest legal reason for doing so, with results that often left the suddenly awakened crusaders with egg on their faces.

The then governor of Ohio, for example, was highly incensed that I did not identify myself as a member of the company's board of directors in every commercial I did on radio and tel-evision. I was delighted to do so because I wanted people to know how much faith I had in our product and how deeply I was involved in protecting policyholders' interests. The public, reassured that I was not merely a figurehead, bought more cov-erage than ever, so much so that we included my board mem-bership in our advertising in all fifty states. I hadn't been trying to hide anything; I had merely felt that it would have been pretentious of me to speak as a director. However, thanks to consumerist zeal that has since greatly diminished because it no longer makes good copy, we were able to extend our coverage to an even greater number of policyholders.

National Liberty Insurance, like any other sound company offering a legitimate service, has ridden out the ministorm of some officials' reactions to our success. It is of no little significance, incidentally, that various insurance commissioners—many of whom were, and are, absolute czars in their domains—who questioned the wording and intent of our advertising were from states harboring old-line companies to whom we were giving the greatest competition. Be that as it may, the company can take care of itself. It is my critics' *unanimous* choice of me as their target that is curious, and to that I wish to address myself publicly for the first time.

There are a number of mail-order insurance companies that offer health benefits similar to those of National Liberty. However, had my critics singled out Company X, whose message was read by a staff announcer in Broken Toe, Utah, they would have received zero press coverage. But attacking Art Linkletter, no matter how spurious and even childish the pretext, was another matter. I was a highly visible, famous target. The question that should be answered, if only for my own satisfaction, is, Why was the whole thing such a big deal?

This is what it all boiled down to. Art Linkletter was asking people to buy insurance without telling them that he was getting paid for it; that was all that emerged from the various trials-by-press-release around the country. Here I was, after over thirty-five years of broadcasting, during much of which I served as spokesman for firms like General Electric and Pillsbury, being accused of being paid for my services! There are, it seems to me, two explanations for this seemingly absurd situation. First, the insurance commercials were extremely believable, not like commercials in the usual sense, simply because I liked what I was selling and knew that it would help a lot of people. I've felt that way about other products I've sold, but this was such a vital matter—my own family holds several policies—that I was able to communicate in a very personal manner.

The second reason that I drew the fire of some public officials has to do with something that I can't possibly change—myself. When a viewer sees Henry Fonda or Sir Laurence Olivier extolling the virtues of a camera or some other product, he doesn't turn to his wife and say, "Gee, if Hank and Larry use those things we better get one because we know they would never take money to tell us about them." In the first place he probably never, even in the privacy of his living room, refers to the two stars as Hank and Larry. They are superstars Henry Fonda and Sir Laurence Olivier doing commercials for such and such. Consciously or subconsciously he may be influenced by their presence—that, after all, is why they are there—but he knows and accepts that they are being paid to say good things about a product that they may or may not personally use.

So along comes Art making his pitch. That's not Arthur G. Linkletter or Mr. Linkletter on the TV screen; that's Art, and I wouldn't have it any other way. Everyone calls me Art with an easy familiarity that the mode of address implies. I know from my mail through the years that people are pleased that Art became a star. It's like one of the family making good. I've always projected that impression because that's the way I relate to people. Consider the title of one of my most popular programs, "People Are Funny." Did anyone take offense at that? Did anyone say, "He's laughing at us" or "Art's making fun of us"? No. Because the audiences knew that I was with them all the way, even as the insurance policyholders knew that I wouldn't knowingly steer them wrong.

I can't help feeling that the rapport I have with middle America was callously exploited during The Curious Affair of National Liberty Insurance by some so-called public protectors because they knew that their names would make the newspapers and the radio and television news shows. Either that or we have a great many imbeciles in positions of public trust; I hardly know which is worse.

I'm not the only television personality to take some heat because of public disagreement over a product. Some years ago Arthur Godfrey was acting as spokesman for a popular detergent when detergents were being hailed as a breakthrough in cleaning technology. Arthur—for some reason "Art" Godfrey doesn't sound right—was doing a tremendous selling job. Then, suddenly, a public agency alleged that his detergent was responsible for all sorts of nasty things, from clogging drains to destroying the ecological balance.

Godfrey, caught in a situation not of his own making, decided that the public agency was right, that his product was doing more harm than good, and, right on the air, quit the account and apologized to his audience for touting something of which he now disapproved. It was a courageous decision, one that I may well have made myself, given the facts.

In an entirely different setting I had to make a decision about my sponsor, and I chose unhesitatingly to defend the company because I believed that my client was right and that any public outcry traced to sometimes deliberately supplied misinformation. I remain associated with National Liberty to this day. One should not from this imply that Arthur was wrong and Art was right, or vice versa. I cite Arthur's experience only to illustrate another performer's involvement in a completely unpredictable controversy, concerning which he must do as his conscience dictates.

Now, briefly, the other side of the coin. I have been disillusioned by the number of people who attempt to defraud National Liberty by falsifying statements about previous illnesses in order to collect large loss claims. I have yet to see or hear an insurance commissioner or any other public official wax indignant over the millions of dollars per year that the voters chisel from the insurance companies. That, one suspects, is because companies can't vote, but people can.

Fortunately, the wonderful relationship between myself and the listeners and viewers that has formed over my professional lifetime is too solidly grounded to be affected by a few months of controversy based on misunderstanding, ignorance, or hypocrisy. If as a young man starting out in San Francisco I had been confronted by the seemingly awesome power of government regulatory agencies, I may have reacted differently as a

National Liberty spokesman. But, then, if I had been that obscure, doubtless the entire matter would not have happened
and the press would never have noticed me.

My indictment ordeal in San Francisco behind me, I was
ready to try for the big time—Hollywood, with all its challenges
and rewards. I broke through into network stardom with "People
Are Funny" on my second try. The story of how I very nearly
lost that show in a sometimes acrimonious behind-the-scenes
struggle with another famous personality, is not generally
known.

Chapter Thirteen

I t will probably come as a surprise that "People Are Funny," the happy show that launched my network career, was born in circumstances anything but joyful.

Two people four hundred miles apart had essentially the same idea for a radio show in 1941: John Guedel, a young Hollywood writer of Hal Roach comedies, and Art Linkletter, a San Francisco radio personality. The format was unique and simple: an entertaining study of human behavior based on a psychologist's observations and reactions. Today the notion of using a psychologist on the air has become so much of a cliché that one tends to forget that someone had to have the initial thought. Using a psychologist, then generally looked upon with a mixture of reverence and suspicion, as a public performer was first discussed seriously in a corner booth at the Brown Derby thirty-five years ago. Whether, in the light of the subsequent inundation of all media by a tidal wave of id probers, our pioneering efforts merit praise or censure I'll leave to the individual reader.

My proposed show was called "Meet Yourself," and my psychologist was at Stanford University. John called his idea "People Are Funny," and his psychologist worked at the University of California, Los Angeles. One would think that the two ideas represented a built-in conflict that could easily result in lawsuits and acrimony extending over many years. Exactly the opposite occurred. John and I met because I had decided to look into the Hollywood scene, and in those days that meant long lunches at the Brown Derby on Vine Street just south of Hollywood Boulevard. We were introduced, talked of our plans, and realized that we had been thinking along similar lines. There was a chemistry between two up-and-coming young men, one a writer-performer and the other a writer-producer, that carried through a professional relationship of more than twenty-five years, and that continues on a personal level to this day.

The Brown & Williamson Tobacco Company was looking for a summer replacement program. John and I worked through two days and nights writing a format for "People Are Funny"—we both agreed that was the better title—and making an audition record, and sent it to the Chicago advertising agency handling the tobacco account. Two days later an agency executive called long distance to say that he would take the show but that he couldn't risk his client's money on an unknown, Art Linkletter. Get a name to work with him and it was a deal.

Guedel and I were ecstatic; our own network show on our first try! John had worked with the popular Art Baker before and arranged that Baker and I become the co-emcees with the emphasis, in the beginning, on him as an established personality. The show went on the air coast-to-coast in June 1941 for Wing cigarettes and really took off in the ratings. By the fourth week three things were apparent: we had a winner, the psychologist was slowing down the pace, and I was much more at ease than the other Art at interviewing people on the microphone. He was a very smooth announcer but not much of an ad-libber. We were getting so many laughs from simply talking to the audience that we decided to eliminate the psychologist, who for all I know went into therapy to overcome his feeling of rejection.

Speaking of rejection. About the fifth or sixth week, when it was becoming obvious that "People Are Funny" was not just another program but a network phenomenon, Art Baker asked me to have dinner with him at Brittingham's, a show-business hangout near the studio. Over coffee he told me very casually that he didn't think we were working out as a team.

I was quite surprised. Between thinking up and writing skits with John and working on mike, I had assumed that everyone was pulling as hard as he could in his own specialty to make the show a success. But I was new to the ways of the big time. Baker said ruefully that one of us had to go, that our personalities didn't mesh. I told him I was sorry he felt that way and that, as co-owner of the show, I'd discuss it with John Guedel.

Guedel and I both agreed that Art Baker's name was an asset, but that if he wanted out there was nothing we could do. By now we were both certain that I could carry the program with a staff announcer to handle the introductions and some commercials. John phoned Chicago to tell the ad execs of the change and to reassure them that the show was now established and everything would go smoothly. What followed was one of the most disillusioning and unhappy experiences of my show-business career.

That, an agency executive replied, was not exactly the way the situation would be resolved. If Art Linkletter and Art Baker couldn't work together, the more well known Art would stay and the fellow from San Francisco would go. Otherwise he felt that his sponsor would not continue with the program.

I was shattered. The agency and the sponsor had heard the show, and my work, for more than four weeks. Surely they must know who was doing the bulk of the interviewing, who was setting up the gags, and, equally important, who, with John, was thinking them up in the first place. I was incredibly naive. Baker, the same white-haired, smiling, friendly fellow you've seen on your home screen, had contacted the agency before he had delivered his ultimatum to me. Knowing that the account executive had sold him to the client in the first place and understanding how insecure most ad-agency people are, Art knew that his threat to withdraw would be enough to shaft me for sure. No agency man would go to his sponsor and say that what he had preached as gospel two months ago no longer applied.

I'll never forget John's loyalty in that most pressing situation. "That does it," he said, "we'll take the show off the air." But I knew that he had put all his financial marbles into "People Are Funny," whereas I was still commuting to San Francisco to carry on my Kaiser and short-wave work and even my man-in-the-street interviews. One night a week I would be a big star in Hollywood on my own network show and the next I would be in Berkeley at the Claremont Hotel emceeing the local quiz program "Do You Want to Be a Genius?" Besides, taking the show off the network would be sheer folly; the agencies and sponsors would never trust us again.

So, for the good of the show, I had to go. And that meant back to San Francisco full time because I had to make a living. For one whole year in San Francisco I wrote material for "People Are Funny," jokes and routines that Art Baker used on the air; it was a galling twelve months in my professional life. Finally, having learned the rules of the game, I knew that the show was established on its own merits beyond doubt. I returned to Hollywood, John Guedel replaced Art Baker with me, and the rest is broadcasting history.

Unfortunately, Baker didn't take the change too gracefully. His background as a song leader and evangelist with Aimee Semple McPherson apparently didn't prepare him to extend Christian forgiveness because he filed a breach-of-contract protest with the American Federation of Radio Artists; it was unanimously rejected by a three-man arbitration panel, one of whose members was chosen by Baker! I was ready to forget about his edging me out, but I think he never quite forgave me for reclaiming my rightful place on my own show.

That character-forming year of "exile" in San Francisco illustrates as well as anything I can think of the kind of toughness of spirit needed to make it and stay on top in show business. I had to live in San Francisco and write material to make the show as good as possible, even though I might never be able to capitalize on its success. I knew that John Guedel was absolutely trustworthy, but I was also aware that there were pressures on him too. My temptation was to forget the whole thing and concentrate exclusively on my safe little Bay Area empire. But I stuck it out and eventually prevailed. Had I failed that crucial test, the chances are good that I would not be writing these words today. That inner strength, derived from guidance beyond myself, again gave me direction.

The trial by fire, the series of minor and major crises that contribute to the making of a star in any entertainment field, is a toughening process that conditions reactions to career situations for the rest of one's life. Show people do not automatically stay on top. Understandably, the public tends to assume that stardom is some kind of divinely bestowed right. Nothing could be further from the truth. A Gregory Peck or a Dinah Shore or a Johnny Carson must exercise unflagging discipline as to choice of material, public image, and free advice from well-meaning associates in order to come up with what is right for him. The greening of Art Linkletter, as described in these pages, is typical of that honing process.

As so often happens, success begets success. A year or so after I rejoined "People Are Funny" John Guedel and I sold "House Party," a half-hour show five days a week on the full CBS network, to General Electric. So began a marathon run on radio and television that extended our successful partnership over so many years.

I've described the amusing, sometimes poignant incidents

connected with those shows at some length in two books, *People Are Funny* and *Kids Say the Darndest Things*. But I've never publicly discussed the inner, personal battles that have accompanied my journey, and I would presume those of other personalities, through life in the public spotlight. What is that man or woman, that star whom you have just paid hard-earned dollars to see in the flesh, thinking before the curtain goes up or the toastmaster completes his introduction? The chief attraction looks so calm and self-possessed, but that's to be expected because, after all, he's a star.

Well, it's not quite that automatic. As I increasingly gained recognition, the invitations to make paid personal appearances began pouring in, as they continue to do, I'm happy to say, to this day. A television or movie star makes those appearances for three reasons: the money, to promote something, or to ensure future fan loyalty—the fan, having seen a star in person, is much more likely to be on hand when that star's new show or motion picture debuts. Some stars dread personal appearances and practically have to be dragged to the theater or auditorium. Others, like myself, enjoy the contact with the public. But even I, having faced live audiences all my life, am susceptible to what I call flop sweat.

Flop sweat is what a performer experiences when, upon entering his hotel room in a medium-size city and looking down at the parking lot that serves the adjoining theater where he is to appear, he sees that the lot is about three-quarters empty ten minutes before show time. There must be another parking lot, he tells himself, and this is the standing-room overflow. As he checks himself in the mirror and heads for the elevator, he knows deep in his heart that there is no other parking lot. He walks backstage, peeks through a spyhole, and sees four hundred people sprinkled throughout a three-thousand-seat theater.

What happened? He must fight off a sense of personal rejection. He *knows* from ratings and fan mail and, equally important, from what the promoter was willing to pay him for this gig that more than four hundred miserable souls wanted to see him in person. The pit band strikes up the overture, the emcee makes his introduction, and . . . he's on.

By now the sparse audience has had time to size each other up, observe all the empty seats, and conclude that somehow each may be a sucker for showing up. The audience is being conditioned to deny the performer the one thing he needs most, reaction.

An audience-participation fellow like me needs response. Telling my jokes is like playing handball; every time I slap a gag out I expect the laughter and applause to bounce back and set me up for the next line. When there is no bounce, when the punch line just lies there suspended and four hundred pairs of eyes stare at me resentfully, it's like a kick in the gut. But on to the next joke. I must go and try again, the while thinking of the egg I'm laying, of the loss the promoter is taking, and of the time my plane leaves for home.

A performer may learn the reason for the sparse crowd too late, after it's all over. Even the biggest name won't draw if the event isn't advertised. Or if the ads appear too late in the local media. Or if the local sponsor, fretting at the big sum he has to pay the star up front, decides to get it back at the box office by charging unrealistic prices. Or, as has happened to me a couple of times, if the star has to compete with a rivalry between two hot baseball teams that are also playing the deciding game of their championship playoff—everyone from the mayor to the theater manager is at the park. Then, too, let's face it, sometimes people just don't show up.

No matter how small or unenthusiastic the audience, I always expect myself and my supporting acts to give it everything we've got. All the more so because these people have paid their money to see us in preference to baseball, or football, or the Academy Awards on television. Our show, booked months in advance by a promoter who could not possibly have foreseen some of the competition, is obliged to thank that audience for showing up by entertaining it as best we can.

Red Skelton tells a classic story of how he once braved a snowstorm to make a personal appearance in a small midwestern town. The storm was so bad that he was the only performer who made it to the theater. Without any music or supporting acts or wardrobe, he went on stage to find that there was only one person in the audience. Red's heart went out to that guy sitting in the front row and he gave the performance of his life—pratfalls, jokes, pantomime, the works. When he was through he walked to the edge of the stage, leaned over the lights, and thanked his solo audience for coming through the storm. The man got up, stretched, nodded, and said not to worry, he lived in the basement; he was the janitor and was just sitting there until Skelton was finished so he could clean up.

My first real baptism with flop sweat occurred in San Francisco's Golden Gate Theater, a vaudeville house where, as the successful emcee of two high-rated radio shows, I was the headline act. In radio the star was protected from an immediate reaction to his show. Ratings took several weeks to trickle back and the studio audience was always SRO because people came in free from all over the country to see what they had been listening to from Hollywood.

When the Golden Gate invited me up for a week's stand and paid me very good money, I figured I had it made. Four shows a day and six on Saturday and Sunday sounded like a bit of a grind but hard work never bothered me. I polished my routines and arrived raring to go.

I had not counted on that vanishing show-biz phenomenon, the vaudeville theater manager. I was suddenly transplanted from the delightful euphoria of a sheltered radio studio where everyone addressed me with either deference or camaraderie, to the chipped-paint domain of a cigar-chewing, stained-vest predator who had managed on the Keith-Orpheum circuit where the really "big" stars like Sarah Bernhardt and Sir Harry Lauder held forth. Furthermore, he informed me, he never listened to the radio.

Beginning at 2 P.M. on week days and 10 A.M. on weekends, we did a live show, had a break while a "C" movie was showing, then did another show, and so on, until closing. We had two types of audience—too few and too many. I can't begin to describe what it feels like to come off stage after a third show to find Neanderthal man waiting in the wings to observe that at this exact time last week Sacha and his French poodles drew three hundred and ten more people; and that two weeks ago, same show time, the Flying Zippos played to capacity. I started to have bad dreams about that manager.

His aggressiveness put me on the defensive and I began to get crafty. "What can you expect," I said after one sparsely attended performance, "the Seals are playing in Sacramento and everyone's up there watching baseball." Or, "It's raining in San Jose and you know that's where the bulk of my listeners are." Or, "There's a traffic jam in the Marina and nobody can get into town." Of course he had heard everything at least fifty times before and knew all the answers.

So much for the small attendance. The house usually was packed on Saturday and Sunday, thanks largely to the fact that kids were out of school. The little darlings would sit through two shows, and surely by the third performance knew every line of my act. I am not given to paranoia, but by the third time that six or eight of them in the front row (they worked their way forward at each audience change) shouted my punch lines in unison I was very near to becoming a basket case.

Over the years I have refined what I like to call "the care and feeding of an audience" down to a fine, ah, art. When I'm introduced I can tell just by the applause what kind of a mood the audience is in, whether it's obligatory applause, desultory applause, enthusiastic applause, or a combination of those basic responses. The vibes coming across the proscenium or up from the banquet tables are, to an experienced speaker, as real as the electronic signals that convert into a picture on your television screen. I know, for example, before the applause has died down whether I'm going to have to open with dynamite material to blast them awake, whether I'm going to toy with them a bit to find the right approach, or whether it's a piece of cake and all I have to do is say "Thank you for that fine introduction" and the house comes down.

Smaller towns especially produce audiences conditioned by my TV image. Often all I have to say is "Good evening," and I get a standing ovation. On the other hand, I've found myself in some really tough situations where I had to summon every learned and instinctive skill to win them over.

One time, at the height of the new drug awareness shortly after Diane's death, I was invited to address a high school assembly in Gary, Indiana. The students were eighty percent black and one hundred percent hostile. Those kids were suspicious, defiant, and cynical. They had been ordered to attend a lecture to be given by an old Hollywood square who, they thought, knew about one-tenth as much as they learned on the street about drugs. When I came on stage and sat down waiting to be introduced, the whole place blossomed with signs and balloons which bore slogans like Light Up and Pot Is Best aimed in my direction.

The school principal, who at six feet five and 280 pounds had obviously been handpicked for the job, introduced me in much the same tones as a prison warden would introduce a new guard. As a matter of fact, now that I think back, it wasn't so much an introduction as an apology, coupled with a thinly veiled threat to give me at least a couple of minutes silence before offing me, I hoped, verbally. For one moment I had a crazy urge to deliver my whole talk from behind the principal but the old professional cool asserted itself and, looking much more at ease than I felt, I came down off the stage and stood level with them on the floor.

There I was, the only person, it seemed, in the hall with a

tie on and no beads, a sort of ritual offering sent by the establishment as a sacrifice to placate the natives.

"I'm glad to be here," I began, "not because of you or the school but simply because someone my age is glad to be anywhere."

Small, grudging titters from widely scattered areas.

"There are a couple of things," I said, "I think we ought to get straight right at the beginning. I haven't come here to lecture you and I haven't come here to tell you not to use drugs. If you want to use drugs, be my guest."

They sat, listening.

"You're the ones who will decide what you're going to eat or drink or put into your bodies. It's not up to me to tell you what to do. If I were your age I'd probably smoke a little grass and do some experimenting, because it's the 'in' thing and I've no doubt to you it's fun and exciting."

Some of them forgot to hold up their signs.

"When I was your age we had something called Prohibition and every kid in my high school who graduated without getting drunk at least once was a sissy."

The laughter came a little more easily. They had decided to let me live.

"Let's talk about drugs," I continued. "Beginning with the two worst, booze and cigarettes."

I could feel the hostility drain away with the breath they exhaled in surprise.

"You've seen your parents get loaded, smoke two packs a day, then come down on you for puffing a little weed. It's a ridiculous double standard, isn't it?"

They applauded, cheered, dropped their signs; and after the cries of "right on" had died away, I told them something about drugs. They listened, the principal told me later, with more attention than he had seen in his four years at the school. I told them, from my experience, what effect drugs had on the human mind and body. When I detected that they were getting restless

I would switch to some anecdote that I knew would recapture their attention, then slide back into my main theme.

My concluding remarks were: "That's all I have to say. You're going to do your own thing, I know that. I just hope that whatever decision you make will be the right one for you. See you around."

I started walking directly toward the exit and was stopped by a standing ovation. It was a great moment, a triumph of experience over circumstances. It enabled me to spread a little knowledge to those youngsters despite themselves.

The main thing when facing a potentially hostile group is to stay loose. The first time I did a show for Warden Clinton Duffy in San Quentin penitentiary I had to change my whole routine in the first two minutes. I stood up in front of nearly four thousand convicts and began my opening monologue. I had forgotten that these guys had a lot of time to listen to the radio and that they had listened to me too faithfully; they knew all my gags.

Soon cries of "Get outta here," "Get some new material," and "You should be in here with us" started drowning me out. What did they care? Was someone going to arrest them for disorderly conduct? My whole show was going up in flames as I waited for the joint—I use the term advisedly—to simmer down. I was thinking about as fast as I've ever thought, and remembered that I was there as part of an annual track meet and spring festival.

"Fellahs," I told them, "I've been talking to the warden about next year's track meet and he's agreed to add an event that I'm sure you'll all want to sign up for." Pause. "It's the cross-country run."

The place came down and I had them with me. Warden Duffy had told me that doing big time made most of the men bitter and resentful; they were all innocent, had been framed, and hated those "guilty" people for being free.

"It's just luck, really," I said, "that I'm here as a visitor because most of us have done something in our lives that qualify us to be sitting right down there with you."

They whistled and stomped their agreement.

"I bet," I continued, "that if you went into any American city, called ten names at random from the phone book, and said, 'The jig is up. It'll be in the papers tomorrow morning,' that nine out of those ten guys would be packed and gone before the morning edition."

They loved it because they chose to believe it, true or not.

On the other hand, there are guaranteed easy audiences. I traveled overseas during the Korean and Vietnam wars to entertain service personnel and their enthusiasm was always so gratifying. The troops didn't want to be there and they knew that I didn't have to be there, so they were eager to show their appreciation. Bob Hope has of course demonstrated time and time again that there are certain buttons to push that are labeled surefire laugh. Officers, food, girls, stateside patriots, draft boards—these and other topics virtually give the performer a free ride on a steady stream of laughter.

One wartime audience, however, I'll never forget, although I suspect that few of those present would recall my visit today. The army asked me to do a show at a large military hospital near Fort Worth, Texas. Despite a tight schedule, I of course accepted. In order to do the show I had to time everything right down to the last minute. I was met at the plane by an officer, whisked to the facility where I had time to shake hands only with the commanding officer before going on in front of a hall full of convalescent soldiers.

I walked out and said, "I'm sure glad to be here," and a whole row of guys toward the back of the hall fell out of their seats laughing.

A soldier in the front row grinned and yelled up reassuringly, "Don't mind them, they're crazy!"

Forth Worth. I didn't see any bandages or wheelchairs or pajamas. It came to me in a flash. A facility for the treatment of battle fatigue, emotional problems, and service-related mental stress. I knew about it from my USO travels, but I simply hadn't put two and two together and realized where I was coming. I was standing there looking down on nearly a thousand guys who through no fault of their own were out of it.

I learned something later that, from my point of view, made the whole appearance even more bizarre. The hall was divided into four sections, ranging from men nearly ready to be released to the newly admitted patients, obviously the section that had responded so effusively to my greeting. That meant four different awareness levels. When I cracked a joke it might appeal to one section, all, or none. I suppose it says something for my performance, though I'm not quite sure what, that before I was through I had all four sections laughing, though never at the same time. A memorable afternoon.

The only comparable experience I ever had was in a vastly different setting with a very different audience, the 1960 Olympic games at Squaw Valley, California. Walt Disney was responsible for the entertainment and was determined to bring to the competitors from all over the world a series of shows that would compete for attention with the games themselves. All the big Hollywood names were at his disposal. Those athletes saw a procession of major stars that even places like Las Vegas today cannot top. Walt lined up the talent and I was in charge of seeing that the headliners actually got on stage. I usually warmed up the audience with a few observations about what had happened in the various meets that day and, in the beginning, with a few jokes.

An act like Danny Kaye, who was sensational, was appreciated in any language. But someone like myself, doing a topical stand-up act, was in a very different position. The various athletes, especially those who didn't understand English, tended to huddle together around their interpreter. Little pockets of audience were scattered all over the large main cafeteria. I would tell a joke, the Americans would laugh, then silence, broken only by frantic whisperings of the one translating my punch line. Finally, like a series of delayed-action bombs, the laughter would begin popping up from widely scattered groups—the Japanese, then the Russians, then the Swedes, then the Portuguese, and so on, as each interpreter finished.

When I addressed the United Nations General Assembly in 1971 on the global nature of the drug problem, I wished that the UN's simultaneous-translation facilities had been at Squaw Valley eleven years earlier. I don't know if it would have gotten me more laughs, but at least the laughter would have come together at once. Incidentally, the UN address was the only speech in my career I have read, and that was only because our State Department had cleared the prepared text to avoid any ad-libs that might create an international incident.

One thing I learned quickly when I began visiting the more conventional service hospitals: patients do not want phony sympathy. Many performers never grasped the men's mood and often came away from well-intentioned hospital tours dismayed and not a little bitter because the patients didn't laugh at their jokes. It takes courage to play to wounded men and women because of the fear—my initial experience at least—of being distasteful and offending them.

It wasn't long, however, before I acquired confidence enough to go into a ward full of multiple amputees and say to men who had no arms, "Well, you guys aren't going to be much of a help with applause." Gallows humor? You wouldn't think so if you could have heard the appreciative laughter. Those men knew that I was there out of sympathy and to help them in my own way. They had done all the thinking they wanted about their problems and their futures and people feeling sorry for them. My presence told them I cared and my jokes set them at ease.

Technically, the absolutely worst place for someone like myself to perform is a large outdoor arena like Veterans Stadium in Philadelphia or the Coliseum in Los Angeles. My type of act usually works from a platform in the center of the field area smack under a bank of huge amplifiers aimed at the four sides of the audience area. In a situation like that I will say "Good evening," pause, and before I can say "ladies and gentlemen," I hear "Good evening" coming at me after a two- or three-second delay bounces it from the speakers to the seats and back again.

All of us, no matter how professional, have little speech mannerisms that go largely unnoticed, even over a sensitive studio microphone. But standing in a huge arena, surrounded by eighty thousand people, I have said, "For our first act, ah, I'd like to . . ." Normally I wouldn't even notice that hesitation, but in a place like Veterans Stadium I've learned to brace myself for the pauses and the AHHHHHHH! Having constantly to talk over the sound of one's own voice repeating what has been said moments before can destroy a performance.

More than once I've attended outdoor political rallies and tried to warn some brash young candidate about local conditions only to be told condescendingly that he has done live network television and can handle a simple speaker setup. I have sat back and, not without a certain glee, watched him begin his address, hear his voice coming back, try again, miss a whole line listening to himself, and then, eyes popping, freeze in front of 50,000 or more prospective voters.

Of all the many thousands of times I have appeared as a performer or guest speaker before almost every conceivable kind of audience, only once did I say "To hell with it" and refuse to perform. Disappointing turnouts, hostile groups, heartrending hospital appearances, six-a-day vaudeville shows—I took them all in my stride until one memorable occasion at Churchill Downs, Kentucky. On the eve of the running of the Kentucky Derby I met my match in the persons of the Kentucky Colonels.

Each year a group of roughly five hundred prominent Derby supporters, who have dubbed themselves the Kentucky Colonels, put on a very elaborate dinner and entertainment to celebrate the next day's race. I had been invited to be toastmaster and general funnyman on this particular occasion and Governor

Happy Chandler was the guest of honor. We were to go full NBC network at 9:00 P.M. By 7:30 the tables were filled and a general spirit of conviviality permeated the hall. At least I guessed that the tables were all filled. I was sitting alongside the governor at the head table and my view was blocked by a high bank of greenery that must have looked most impressive from down front.

The green shield didn't bother me too much because I knew that when I stood I would at least be visible from the shoulders up. It was only when I noticed that the greenery was moving that I began to grow a little concerned. What I was seeing was a continuous parade of waiters' trays held aloft and carrying an endless belt of mint juleps down to the thirsty Colonels. By 8:15 Governor Chandler and I were screaming at each other to make ourselves heard over the rising din. I have spoken at conventions of salesmen and to gatherings of show-business celebrities, two breeds that tend to register many decibels of alcoholic hilarity, but I have never experienced anything remotely approaching that gathering. The Kentucky Colonels were getting into the bag as our air time approached.

The din was so overwhelming that when the NBC engineer frantically gave us a cue and Ed Pauley, who was sitting on my left, rose to introduce me, I couldn't hear what he was saying. On my right Happy Chandler was more than living up to his nickname, trying to keep me from feeling left out with a steady barrage of comments on everything from the international scene to his plans to run for higher office.

While watching Ed's mouth move to be sure that he was still talking and trying to be polite to an increasingly jovial governor, I was thinking about what happened in this same place the previous year. George Jessel had been the emcee and, like any good pro, had put himself right on the line when he was introduced. He would wait, he told the Colonels, until they quieted down so he could make himself heard. Well, they didn't quiet down, ever, and the whole thing was a disaster.

Ed Pauley sat down so I presumed I had been introduced. I stood without the slightest hint of recognition from the mob. They weren't even aware that there had been a change in speakers. I was supposed to do eight to ten minutes of standup jokes. I looked out over the vast sea of cockeyed Colonels, said, "Thank you, Mr. Pauley. Now here is your first speaker, Governor Happy Chandler," and sat down.

Happy, apparently oblivious to the lack of response, made a speech. When he was finished I introduced the mayor, and so on down the list of dignitaries until we had used up our air time. I didn't crack a single joke or make any other kind of comment. Yet when I was trying to escape from the head table, a number of boisterous Colonels cornered me and said that I was even funnier in person than on the air. One chap said that he had heard me in person before, but that tonight had to go down as the greatest performance of my career. A thoroughly unpleasant experience.

On one other occasion I failed to make a scheduled appearance. On October 5, 1969, one hour before I was to address the Air Force Academy graduating class in Colorado Springs, Colorado, my son Robert called me from California to tell me that his sister, my beautiful nineteen-year-old Diane, was dead.

Chapter Fourteen

I don't think I'd want to know that something terrible is going to happen to me."

That's Diane's voice. Now, eleven years after her death, I can listen. She made that remark on her radio interview show barely one month before she died. Intuition, prescience, coincidence? I neither know nor care. She would send me tapes of her broadcasts so I might catch up on those I had missed because I was away on personal appearances. They remained stacked in my den, untouched, until recently. It occurred to me that, through her words, I might help the reader understand her better.

As most of the world seems to know, Diane was killed as the result of a fall or jump from the sixth-floor balcony of her Hollywood apartment above the Sunset Strip. It made for a legitimate news story that, painful though it was to Lois and me, we were prepared to accept. The inevitable sniffing for possible scandal because my daughter was involved was more difficult to take. The scandal was there for all to see. Apparently possessed of some drug-induced demon that made her by turns calm and emotionally unstable, Diane ended her life.

No measurable amount of any drug was found in her system after her death.

That's an important sentence that I trust helps put to rest some innuendos and malicious rumors. I can only speculate, from information supplied me by some of her friends later, that she had taken LSD in the past and had experienced a flash or recurring bad trip identified with that most insidious hallucinogen. An acid trip is a trip straight to hell. No matter if the initial experience is "good" or "bad"—if the experimenter sees, hears, and smells pleasant things or is sent crashing into a world of unspeakable horrors—it is acid's tendency to repeat that makes it such a powerful force.

One day, one month, one year, or ten years from its original ingestion, acid can strike with literally dizzying suddenness—in the time it takes to walk across a kitchen floor—and turn a rational, composed individual into a raving lunatic.

There was a young man with Diane the evening she died. He recalled to the police and my private investigators that she began feeling something wrong while she was cooking dinner for them both. She telephoned her brother Robert, fearful that she was having the start of a recurring bad trip; her companion got on the phone and told my son not to worry, that he had Diane in sight all the time, and that he would make certain that she didn't hurt herself.

Robert and Diane, my two youngest, had always been close, and Robert hung up the phone in an unsettled frame of mind. He knew that Diane had gone through one previous unpleasant recurrence. Although he trusted the young man who was with his sister, he decided to go to her apartment, just to be safe. As he was driving over, Diane had settled down. She left her friend in the living room to go into the kitchen and check the oven. No one saw her alive after that.

Whatever it was must have hit her as she crossed the kitchen—the chocolate cookies she was making lay unbaked beside the oven—and caused her to detour to a sliding-glass exit onto the balcony. Within seconds she had plunged to her death.

One year earlier I had been warned that Diane was mixing with undesirable, perhaps drug-oriented young people. Pack trips into the mountains have long been a family tradition. We would all get together and head into some remote area removed from contact with the outside world. There we would simply have fun as a family, enjoying nature and generally becoming reacquainted with one another, free from the constant pressures of my profession.

Diane invited her current boyfriend to join us on one occasion, and it was soon obvious to everyone that he had really fallen for her. The young man didn't realize that my youngest daughter could project a sense of intimacy and togetherness the way other people shake hands, and unhappily for him do it with the same casualness. In short, Diane liked to flirt. She had all the equipment to keep prospective suitors standing in line. Blessed with a pretty face, a cute figure, and an outgoing personality, she had two other assets: the knowledge that as my daughter she attracted attention, and the ability to put her natural and acquired advantages to work for her.

I enjoyed watching her. She was vibrant, aware of her power, and loved to parade her love-sick trophies for my inspection. So when this particular young man on the pack trip took me aside solemnly to warn me about Diane's suspect friends, I was inclined to discount some of his concern. Especially when he pointed out that as long as she was in his company I need have no worries.

Nevertheless, I did ask her about her companions and she readily admitted that there was some pot smoking going on but that surely I knew her better than to think she could be pushed into anything that she didn't want to do. She denied being involved in any drug experimentation and promised that she would never do anything that "stupid." She told her mother that there were some parties she was afraid to attend because of heavy drug use.

What does a man do when his daughter stands there and tells him she isn't doing anything wrong? He believes her, particularly in the absence of any proof to the contrary. I felt quite certain she couldn't be forced into any bad situation against her will. What I failed to take into account was that, as my daughter, she wanted to show that she was just a regular gal and might even take the initiative to prove it.

So it appears that Diane lied to me, and in fact had been on at least one acid trip. I don't know how, after the fact, I could have behaved any differently. My subsequent investigations established she was what is called a "spree user," someone who tries something new on a casual, devil-may-care basis, usually at a weekend party or perhaps on a dare. She was by no means a regular user.

Diane's tragedy is that perhaps only one adventure with LSD came back to haunt her and take her life. Although I have come full circle in my thinking about much drug use, I remain adamant in my condemnation of acid. It is an unpredictable, strong drug that strikes without warning to cause either self-destruction or, in the case of the notorious Manson murders, a distorted awareness of an alleged need for violence toward others.

In the months immediately following Diane's death I was at one with my late father's teaching, "Vengeance is mine; I will repay, saith the Lord," appointing myself as His earthly deputy. Nor was I alone. A very good friend of mine, a prominent motion-picture and television star whose name is a household word, came to me one night with a suggestion not at all in keeping with his professional image. Both in public and in private he is a compassionate individual, given to make people laugh at their own foibles rather than to advocate violence.

"Art," he said, "what happened to Diane is the top of the volcano blowing off. You and I know that the drug pushers regard the area we live in as their greatest sales outlet. Celebrities' children are doubly vulnerable, their names make them open targets, and they have the money to spend on drugs."

As I think back on that evening I find it difficult to believe that this star who has done so much to help others in trouble through free charity appearances and private donations could have suggested what he did. Yet there was no doubt that he was in earnest; his voice trembled in his rage as he spoke to me in my den.

"Do these pushers, this filth, get justice even if they're caught? No. They have money to pay fines and too often they get off with a light sentence or probation and hours later they're back down near the school or over in the park selling to our kids. Art, let's five or six of us put in ten thousand dollars each, set up a bank account, and hire some top private investigators to identify the key pushers, the ones who are essential to all the smaller operators. We'll only go for the big shots, without whom a lot of the street business would fold."

"And then what," I asked, "turn them over to the police or the DA for prosecution?"

"No," his voice dropped almost to a whisper. "We go out and kill them ourselves."

I stared at him in silence. This gentle man who would never permit words like that to be put into one of his scripts was completely serious.

"We . . ." For once words eluded me. "We couldn't do anything like that," I finally managed.

"Why not? We're all so well known that we'd be above suspicion. The very idea that we would do anything like that would be considered so absurd that no one would even dream of investigating us." He had obviously thought the whole thing out. "And the good we would do; others would be afraid to take their place because they'd think there was some kind of mob war going on. We'd save not only our kids, Art, but thousands of other youngsters throughout this whole area."

Perhaps my friend's idea seems farfetched, aside from its illegal and immoral aspects. But the fact that he would even
suggest it, that I had actually to discourage him in his plan, gives
you some idea of the near panic climate that faced many of us
in the Holmby Hills–Bel Air–Beverly Hills areas in those drug-
crazed days.

I would be dishonest if I implied that a sense of Christian
charity prompted me to dissuade my friend from his extermi-
nation proposal. But there are some absolutes in this world and
not committing murder is one of them. My mind turned to a
more practical method—which also was both legal and Christian—of neutralizing the drug-selling underworld; I would take
my best shot, metaphorically speaking, and use my God-given
ability to communicate with people.

So I ranged across the nation, taking advantage of the media
coverage of our tragedy, to speak out against everything from
pot to heroin everywhere from the Wichita Chamber of Commerce to the Oval Office in the White House. I was trying to
avenge Diane and to repay the public for their sympathy.

I will never forget that terrible night of her death. After flying
back from Colorado Springs, Lois, Dawn (my eldest daughter),
and I were walking across the reception area of Los Angeles
International Airport where we were met by people who, with
tears in their eyes, impulsively grabbed my hand and said they
were sorry. These weren't autograph seekers or fans anxious to
have their presence noticed; they were simply people who
wanted us to know they really cared.

My God, I remember thinking as I rubbed the moisture from
my own eyes, I know for the first time what "I'm sorry" really
means. Since then I have never used those words without a
special personal commitment to the sorrowing. Today that commitment is too often missing in the ritual expressions of sympathy. The coldly commercial atmosphere of a busy metropolitan
airport is probably a strange place to witness His compassion
through the eyes and words of fellow Christians. I felt God's

presence that night shielding my wife, my daughter, and myself as we rushed toward a waiting car. It's all right, Art, something told me; this is one you won't have to fight by yourself.

During the past few years my views on the marijuana and other drug problems have softened considerably as time eased my hurt and reason reasserted itself. I do not feel that smoking a little weed is certain to send anyone to degradation's depths and I'm not even certain where criminal prosecution should begin. What, for example, is a pusher? A pusher quite often is a financially strapped user. The user sells to friends to finance a habit. I think a distinction should be made between that kind of transaction and the coldly calculating wholesalers who import the drug in quantity, spread it into the streets, and knowingly encourage people to turn on in order to increase the market.

Some well-meaning people would have us attack the problem from the other end and try to cure the habit. In the case of heroin addicts, the use of methadone as a "harmless substitute" invariably crops up. Putting a heroin user on methadone is, in my opinion, like taking a cripple off crutches and sitting him in a wheelchair. There, we are saying in effect, you still can't walk by yourself but we've changed your support system. It is no coincidence that methadone is now a drug of choice on the street market.

A recent report by the General Accounting Office, an investigative arm of Congress, reveals the startling information that more than sixteen hundred deaths occurred from methadone abuse in the past two years. Methadone is getting on the street with increasingly devastating results.

We only have to remember how heroin came into being to understand the proliferation of deadly methadone. Morphine was called the soldier's drug during the Civil War because its application by the newly invented hypodermic needle eased battlefield pain, but it also created an army of addicts during the postwar period. How to stem the rising addiction? The Bayer Company came up with a substance it called heroin (from the

Greek *heros*), which was guaranteed to "cure" morphinism. Substitute methadone for heroin and another link lengthens the lethal chain that holds the addict mind and body in demoniacal bondage.

The problem of proliferating drug use admits of no simple solution, and I confess that I despair of it being solved in my lifetime. Although I believe that ingesting any foreign substance for the purpose of altering emotional attitudes is wrong—and I firmly believe that—I do not feel that harsh criminal penalties for those who are essentially victims are helping the situation. A better understanding of the weaknesses of others is indicated. In my own case, for example, I neither drink nor take pills because I have no need to. I have few anxieties, am "up" for a show or a business deal, and am able to enjoy my leisure time without any artificial aids. I have to be very careful not to condemn, even subconsciously, friends and business associates who take a couple of belts at the end of the day to relax themselves. If a drink helps them, so be it. And I think the same attitude should apply to those who make marijuana their emotional crutch. I will never say that getting loaded or spaced out is a proper, natural human condition because I do not believe it is. But those who must so immunize themselves from life's problems and challenges should not necessarily be regarded as criminals.

Suppose Diane had been busted for possession. Would I have regarded her as a criminal or as merely a strong-willed, mischievous young girl out to sample as much of life as she could? My thoughts of Diane may be so subjective that the reader might wonder if I'm giving a total picture. So, with her permission, I'm going to quote a brief passage from a letter Dawn, my eldest daughter, who lives at Lake Tahoe in Northern California, wrote to Lois shortly after Diane's funeral.

"I'll never forget the three of us [in a hotel room in Colorado Springs] hanging on to one another and crying. Daddy seemed so vulnerable, a strange word to use in connection with him.

I've been thinking about that ever since, and how he might be blaming himself for something he really couldn't help. Diane was looking for something, I don't know what because we were never really close, but I can think way back seeing my kid sister clearly as being very aware.

"Remember when she was the flower girl at my wedding? She couldn't have been more than nine; I can see her now with her hair in a ponytail, swinging it back and forth as she walked that saucy walk of hers around the pool. Parents don't always understand but some girls are sexy practically the day after they're born. Diane was like that. She was a natural flirt, climbing up into men's laps and hugging them when she was only five or six.

"I remember thinking, even then, 'That little girl is going to chase after something in life. I hope no one gets hurt.' "

Dear, wonderful, compassionate Dawn. Both Lois and I did see those traits in Diane, but who could have predicted where they would lead, if in fact those characteristics had anything to do with what happened? What were Lois and I to say? Stop being outgoing, alter your walk, don't be flirtatious, curb your ambition. Only a fool would try to suppress the spirit and liveliness of a pretty young girl. We were proud of her and remain so. Nothing will ever change that.

Diane was well on her way to achieving prominence in show business. She had her radio show and was all signed up to appear on television in the fall of 1970. Just months before her death she and I had made a record, "We Love You, Call Collect," aimed at the then current trend of kids running away and trying to find themselves in the drug-oriented subculture. The record won a Grammy Award, and she had recently returned from a trip publicizing it on radio and television. I have heard that there are stories implying that I somehow used her death to exploit the sales of that record. Even as I write this I can't conceive the sick minds who could believe, let alone circulate, a rumor like that. But I'm told that it persists to this day.

The record *was* reissued after Diane's death, but I had nothing to do with it. I suppose, in retrospect, I could have tried to get a restraining order or some such thing, although I doubt that I could have stopped the company from going ahead. Again in retrospect, what harm did it do? I would even venture a guess that some kids listening to her voice after her death might have awakened to the fact that they were playing with dynamite and opted to save their own lives by going home. As for the tremendous profits I'm supposed to have reaped, I can only say that the returns from the recording were so minimal that we didn't even bother to include them in the Diane Linkletter Fund that Linkletter Enterprises, a multi-million-dollar corporation, established after her death.

Incidentally, anticipating the weirdos who would imply that I might try in some way to capitalize on my daughter's death, I arranged that the Fund be administered by the School of Medicine at the University of California, San Francisco, which already had an ongoing drug-abuse prevention program. Had I set up a private foundation there would doubtless have been those who, having the latest inside word, would charge that I was channeling money from it to myself. UCSF was, I hoped, above suspicion.

Earlier I said that I have never been bitter about setbacks in my professional career. I cannot help, however, being resentful at the way some soulless individuals pounce on the misfortune of a young girl to vent their jealousies and frustrations. These faceless, formless rumormongers exist in a shadow world of vitriol and hate. Perhaps some day on a camping trip to the place where Diane used to scramble happily under the towering pines, I'll turn over a rock and see what one looks like.

Chapter Fifteen

But let us speak of happier times. I suppose, in quoting from Dawn's letter to her mother, it is only fair that I include other passages that Lois feels are pertinent.

"I remember that swimming pool, the first we ever had, so well," Dawn wrote. "We were all so excited and Daddy so proud. He bought one of those war-surplus rubber dinghys that you blow up. He used to sit in it with his typewriter and float around for hours at a time working on his scripts. I can still see him typing away, floating day after day."

Christmas dinner at Dawn's has become a family tradition and all of us do a lot of skiing at that time. I was very sports-oriented in college; two sports, swimming and basketball, I especially liked. As the starting center on a basketball team today I would be "protected" from raids by coaches of other sports at my college. But in those days it was every coach for himself. If a student looked reasonably healthy and had all four limbs, he stood a good chance of being "invited" to try out for any team.

As I was not only healthy, but also an accomplished swimmer and a first-string center, it was inevitable that I should be tapped by the football coach, a circumstance I viewed with some apprehension. At six feet two and around two hundred pounds I was no midget, but I had watched the mayhem referred to euphemistically as a practice scrimmage and could see my basketball days cut short by a broken something. So when the various positions on the football team were being filled I hung back, watching for the one that nobody wanted. I figured that all the hotshot athletes would volunteer for the action spots. I was right. Only another chap and I turned out for center. What a choice!

I still have cleat marks up and down my back memorializing that disaster. I'd snap the ball and my quarterback would use me as a bridge to fame and fortune. Or I would be defending and the guy opposite me would make me a carpet for *his* quarterback. One year of football was enough for me. Fortunately our varsity basketball team took preference in my senior year, and as team captain, I played every minute of every game in a season that took us to the Southern California championship of our college conference.

In later years I played four-wall handball, an extremely demanding sport requiring a running back's stamina and a shortstop's hands. With the introduction of glass walls, handball is only now beginning to achieve proper recognition. Before that, only a few people could watch a game because they had to peer down over one end of the court. Now, with glass walls, the potential audience jumps from thirty to thirty million, as television, for the first time, can cover the intricacies and excitement of competitive play.

When I was fifty a bad knee forced me to give up handball. Although I swam every day in our pool at home, I felt out of the action because I had always been a very physical person. That's when Lowell Thomas came to my rescue. We were at the Bohemian Grove, a private club situated over a sprawling nest of redwood groves sixty-five miles north of San Francisco. Founded in 1880, the club yearly hosts what is probably the most impressive gathering of national leaders that could be brought together anywhere in the world. The biggest names in finance, industry, show business, and politics gather in the club's informal atmosphere to exchange ideas and have a good, relaxing time.

Lowell, then in his middle sixties, told me how much he enjoyed skiing and invited me to join him later that year in Sun Valley. I had to admit that I didn't know how to ski and, at fifty and with an uncertain knee, wasn't sure that I wanted to learn. He shamed me by comparing our ages, and so began a wonderful new adventure for myself, Lois, whom I taught later, and the children. I took some time off from writing this book to ski with Lowell, now in his eighties, and we both agreed that we were just warming up to challenge faster hills in the years ahead.

Which leads me to another statement in Dawn's letter, on which, in deference to the equal-time doctrine, I feel compelled to comment. She writes of her enthusiasm for skiing and of the great times we have every Christmas, then adds: "Daddy doesn't like anyone to see him fall down."

Probably she's referring to an occasion when I deliberately threw myself out of the way of a neophyte on short skis to avoid a bruising collision. Actually I did have one experience on skis prior to my talk with Lowell Thomas and it made me all the more leery of ever getting on those long slats again. You will recall that I was coordinating all the entertainment for the 1960 Olympic games at Squaw Valley, where the name of the game, literally, was skiing. One day Walt Disney suggested that I try the slopes myself.

Well, you have to get the picture. I was very conscious of my high visibility as a celebrity, but I could not turn away from a challenge that involved sports. For once my gut reaction took precedence over my good sense, so I strapped on a pair of six-foot-ten-inch skis. I ruled out an instructor's suggestion that I begin on a practice hill about the height of a pitcher's mound. Art Linkletter, television star, athlete, and all-round success symbol, was not about to be seen pigeon-toeing it down some sissy mound with the girls and young kids.

So up the lift I went, smiling and waving as the other skiers yelled their welcome. The first thing I realized when I got to the top was that the laws of physics had somehow been suspended for the Olympics. The hill was definitely longer and steeper looking down than it was looking up. With the approving cries of some fans echoing in my ears, I dug in my poles and pushed off. There are few things more amusing than a beginning skier fighting to retain his balance and losing the battle—if you're not the skier.

I had scarcely left the lip of the hill when, one ski wildly flailing the air as I desperately fought for control, I flipped over and skied the entire hill on my back, my skis thrashing wildly over my head and my parka filling with snow scooped up on the way down. I was making my getaway plans as I came to rest ignominiously against a tree in a snowbank right next to the line waiting to board the lift. Two ladies came rushing over, stared at me, and without my having anything to write on or with, asked me for my autograph. Those two came very close to getting a Linkletter ad-lib guaranteed to stop cold the bridge club back home. "Art said that?" I can hear them asking in Cleveland.

Skiing has since become an integral part of my life. The annual Art Linkletter family ski race, held at Alpine Meadows in Northern California, is, I believe, the only event of its kind where entire families, from youngest to oldest, compete and the scores are averaged out. The race typifies for me what sports are all about, a physical activity for fun with some competition. I do not hold with what sports have become in this country, namely, an event in which winning is everything and second place is a disgrace. That tenet parallels our general preoccupation with materiality. Forgetting the fun in sports is like forgetting God in our daily lives; both the reason for doing something and the reason for existing are distorted and become essentially meaningless.

On a practical level, sports have been instrumental in my not smoking or drinking. Anything that might upset my coordination or break my concentration is anathema to me. I cannot see the enjoyment in skiing a slope while half gassed, to say nothing of the danger to both the skier and anyone who has the misfortune to get in his way.

I do not believe myself to be a great natural athlete. I am not as well coordinated as, and I don't have the moves of, people with naturally quick reflexes. I have excelled at some sports only because I have been doggedly persistent in my quest for something as near to perfection as I am capable of achieving.

That word *persistence* is the key to my whole survival ethic. If I have made my mark in the entertainment field, in business, and, in a more private way, in sports, it is because I persisted often when others of equal or superior ability fell by the wayside. A canceled sponsor, a dry oil well, an inglorious slide down a ski slope on my rear end—each setback spurred me on to try again and do better.

I sometimes feel that if Diane, for example, had tried to make her grades and stay in college she might not have been distracted by superficial relationships. Had she persisted and graduated, perhaps she would have achieved the maturity that she clearly did not have at the time of her death. I've been replaying some of her tapes as I sit here and I hear her saying things like this:

"College was a bust for me. I really didn't dig college. I found that when I went to college—I'm not being cocky—but because I've been raised in theater, I found that they were teaching me stuff I already knew. And, like it was really a drag."

Really a drag. The irony is, that mode of speech was foreign to her; it was her way of relating to kids who were not daughters of celebrities, her way of showing them that she was no snob.

And there was obviously some "stuff" about which she knew little or nothing. What even more discourages me is the thought that I might not have been capable of giving her the answers she sought, had she come to me with whatever questions she had about her acquaintances and their lifestyles.

Norman Vincent Peale, trying to comfort me, said that Diane's death may have been God's way of arousing me so that I could reach out and alert hundreds of thousands of other youngsters to the dangers of ingesting substances like acid; in effect, swapping one life for who knows how many. I don't know. I'm just glad that God didn't ask me to make that conscious choice. I'm afraid I would have let Him down.

Chapter Sixteen

It is not generally known that I have been approached many times to run for political office. Everything from the mayor of Los Angeles to governor and senator has been suggested by groups of friends commanding enormous financial resources. These have not been idly speculative propositions. I have been offered unlimited funds —"whatever it takes"—in support of my candidacy. I stress the seriousness of the proposals to underscore the soberness of my refusals. Faith so earnestly expressed is not easily denied.

The arguments in favor of my going into public life have usually been twofold: "Everybody likes Art Linkletter"; and the administrative abilities that have made me a business success lend themselves to high political office.

Let's, for the sake of argument, suppose that the first statement is true. My response is that the first time I enter the political arena I automatically risk a lifetime of pleasant relationships with the public: many of the people hearing my announcement will immediately begin to have doubts about me. Will they not wonder about an apolitical entertainer who helped folks forget their troubles and gave them a few laughs along the way becoming the party's nominee? I'm going to make somebody mad, no matter what I say. Indeed, even if I say nothing, some folks will find fault, as Jimmy Carter learned during the early stages of his first presidential campaign.

Having in one stroke largely repudiated a jealously protected public image, I proceed to the second statement. Business and executive ability has little import on a candidate's ability to win elections. Political debate is shot through with evasions and half-truths, neither of which I'm very good at. I think that most people, even those whose well-meaning letters through the years prompt this explanation, would prefer knowing me as I am to being dismayed by the realization that I could not simultaneously be both Republican and Democrat. I yield to no one in my devotion to small children, dogs, Abraham Lincoln, motherhood, and the American flag, but I choose to help my country as best I can in the role of a private citizen, through example, charities, and my influence with elected officials.

High government office has been available to me without the rigors of a political campaign but I turned down those opportunities on principle; if I would not compete democratically for public office, I would certainly not slide in through an appointive side door, no matter how flattering the prospective position. This is not to condemn those who serve as appointed officials; the nation could not function without them. Appointive office is simply not my particular cup of tea.

I use that last expression with good reason because it reminds me of Australia and of the American ambassadorship there that was offered to me by President Nixon and respectfully declined.

I've known Dick Nixon for over twenty years. We've appeared at many head tables together. Bob Hope and I have emceed a large number of fund raisers for him, including one memorable occasion when, at a thousand-dollar-a-plate dinner, we raised more than one million dollars in a single evening. I'm as puzzled by as I am disappointed at the events surrounding Watergate because they suggest to me a very different man from the Nixon I know both as a public and as a private person.

I was an emcee at both presidential inaugurals as well as at the celebrated party at the Palladium on Sunset Boulevard when Nixon, smarting from his defeat in the race for governor of California, told the reporters that they wouldn't have Dick Nixon to kick around any more. I've seen him in triumph and defeat, and know him to be possessed of that quality I find so admirable in successful leaders, persistence, the ability to roll with the punch.

I first realized that there was more to the man than simply a politician seeking public office when in 1967, as a fellow member of the Bohemian Grove, he gave an impromptu talk to a group that included several former ambassadors, college presidents, and the heads of many of our largest banks and corporations. We were all sprawled informally on the ground beside a lake as Dick Nixon, without any prepared script, took us on an imaginary world tour. Country by country, he reviewed the political and economic relationships to the United States, going from the recent past to the present and then forecasting probable developments and courses of action. It was a virtuoso performance. Very few men would have dared to attempt in front of such a knowledgeable audience what he did. The applause had a special significance, because it was in large measure as a result of that talk that a group of influential citizens offered to back Dick in a bid for the presidency. The shy, retiring introvert, dubbed "Gloomy Gus" by his college classmates, forced himself once again to assume an outgoing public posture and was, of course, elected in 1968.

The following year, two months after Diane's death (my life in a very real way has become divided into "before" and "after" Diane), I was in the White House as the President's overnight guest. He had previously offered me the post of ambassador to Australia and asked me if I had made a decision. I was in something of a quandary. One does not lightly turn down a personal request by the President, yet, during this period of escalating drug use by our nation's youth, I had very strong feelings about my place in the scheme of things. I answered the President's question with one of my own: Did he think I would better serve the nation by representing it in Australia or by devoting my time and energy to combating the very real drug threat at home and trying to make our young people aware of the peril?

The President reflected for some time before breaking the silence. He agreed with my private belief that helping a new generation cope with a pervasive, potentially destructive force was more important. I must for the record state that at no time since I have known Dick Nixon have I been aware of any excessive drinking by him or, most particularly, of his supposed habitual use of foul language. I've searched my memory, recalling the times I've dined with him and Pat in the family dining room upstairs in the White House, and I can't remember his even having a highball before dinner. I have sat with him many times in the Oval Office, just the two of us, and the worst thing I have heard him say was son-of-a-bitch, and that only once, when he learned that a minor functionary had given an unauthorized press conference conveying erroneous information that threatened to louse up one of our drug programs.

One of my fondest memories has the President, in a rare moment that revealed the little-boy side of him, pressing concealed switches in the wall molding, causing hidden doors to swing open to secret passages and staircases used by past Presidents to move unnoticed from one part of the White House to another. Probing around, I inadvertently pressed a hidden latch revealing an undiscovered passage. Delighted, the President swung the door wide and dislodged a heavy picture that I caught only inches from his head. He might well have been knocked cold. I still feel somewhat uneasy when I think of my having to summon the Secret Service to help revive the President.

I was in both Haldeman's and Ehrlichman's company a number of times and experienced none of the so-called Prussian ruthlessness generally attributed to them. Ehrlichman, particularly, I found to be a gracious, intelligent man and acutely aware of the outside world. I realize, however, that there are two very good reasons why I was well received: I was the President's personal friend and, perhaps more important, I was absolutely no threat to anyone on the staff.

Intelligent people who are willing to give Richard Nixon the benefit of the doubt remain troubled by the caliber of some of the men under him. I do not share that uncertainty because I can explain the relationships by my own experience. Most busy, active executives have to delegate authority; they welcome subordinates who are ready to respond to their business needs anytime, with total dedication. It becomes easier to rely on assistants who are instantly available and of unquestioned, though sometimes misguided, loyalty than to utilize the services of others who, though perhaps more capable, are not as accessible. And that, I believe, is in the main what happened to Richard Nixon.

The public so easily forgets the many difficult and, as it so often turned out, right decisions he made as President. I was with him when he decided to go ahead with the controversial policy of bombing Cambodia. "Art," he told me, "I know how this is going to be received by the press. I know that it may well result in my personal, to say nothing of the Republican party's, fall from favor. It could put us out of office for many years. But it's the right thing to do." He paused and waved his hand for emphasis. "It's going to shorten this war and that's the important thing, the right thing, and I'm going to do it." That's the Richard Nixon I remember.

My career has afforded me the fascinating opportunity of meeting a large cross section of people. For example, during the initial months of my drug-oriented speeches and travels I visited, within a few days, Richard Nixon, President of the United States, and Nicky Cruz, former president of one of the most vicious bands of young Puerto Ricans that prowled the Brooklyn streets and alleys in the early 1960s.

Nicky emerged as the leader of his nearly three hundred followers because he was tougher than anyone else. When one realizes that the gang was composed of knife specialists quite capable of committing murder, Nicky's prowess is all the more remarkable. He and his troops were a potent force for evil that would have gone unchecked had it not been for the Reverend Dave Wilkerson, the legendary street missionary. Nicky and Dave, a most unlikely pairing, met in the streets and there, with the churchman's help, the gang leader found God.

Then an even more impressive strength flowed into the young Puerto Rican and he worked to turn the gang members away from drugs and violence. Today he embraces the volatile, fast-spreading charismatic Christian movement and remains one of the more memorable individuals with whom I have come into contact.

My work with World Vision International and its dynamic head, Stan Mooneyham, has been especially rewarding as a means of spreading Christian ideas and beliefs. World Vision is a charitable foundation that helps people in need by building schools and hospitals, reestablishing farms, relocating refugees, and arranging for needy youngsters to be "adopted," as it were, by remote control by sponsoring Americans. As a spokesman, I travel around the world making documentary films of steps being taken to ease suffering in places like Cambodia and Bang-ladesh.

Although my work for World Vision represents a contribution of time and talent to a worthwhile cause, it is surprising how strictly commercial enterprises can turn into public-service un-dertakings that bring much happiness to people. Everyone knows about Bob Hope's annual Christmas junkets to entertain troops abroad. Although he has discontinued the trips, they represented a perfect blending of patriotic and commercial motivation. The armed forces saw shows that they could not see stateside and Bob's sponsors got themselves an entertaining, highly rated television special every year.

What most people do not know is that while Bob was traveling around the globe entertaining servicemen, I was home having fun with their wives. Don't jump to the wrong conclusion!

It all began when I was retained by Harrell International to promote Formula 409, a new kitchen cleaner. I toured the country making personal appearances and doing commercials. We did so well that we found ourselves in an all-out advertising war with Procter & Gamble, which had introduced its own cleaner, Cinch. P & G deigned not to bring its big guns to bear on us, treating our relatively small campaign as an isolated encounter. We managed to beat P & G, outselling its product and establishing 409 as the choice of millions of housewives.

Beating Procter & Gamble even when it wasn't looking was quite an achievement, and board chairman Wilson Harrell asked me to act as the company spokesman in another large phase of its operation, selling to military PXs and commissaries around the world. The military outlets were important for three reasons: the large sales volume, their use as a testing ground for products about to be introduced to the domestic market, and the establishing of buying habits among thousands of service families that would eventually return home.

Mine was essentially a goodwill mission because the hard commercial sell was taboo in military areas. We relied heavily on POP (Point of Purchase) inducements and my visiting everyone from the camp commanders to the supply sergeants was designed to enhance the company image and encourage product display. But I realized on my very first trip to Great Britain that I simply couldn't do it that way. Set me down in the middle of a crowd of women and kids who are appreciative of my coming all that way to visit and I want to entertain them. I was being paid for all this yet I felt I was giving nothing to my audience, so I did a miniature "House Party" right there in an air force base commissary. I started with an opening monologue, told a few jokes, and worked simple stunts with some of the kids and their mothers. Both the dependents and the army brass loved it and wrote enthusiastic letters to the Harrell company.

Wilson Harrell suggested that I take along a camera crew next time to film what happened so he could show it to sales conferences across the country. I wondered aloud that if we were going that far, why not take a full shooting crew with several cameras and sound to do a series of complete television shows. We realized right then that no one had ever taken a show on tour specifically to entertain the service wives and children, and from that realization emerged our Military Wife of the Year Award.

I sent some of my advance people ahead to scout for wives with interesting stories or experiences; we soon found that among the hundreds of thousands of dependents was a vast untapped reservoir of material. Sight unseen, I sold the idea to CBS for a big special in the days when "specials" were just that. As we moved from base to base it was obvious that the news of our coming had spread. What began as a few off-the-cuff stunts near a commissary check-out stand blossomed into a full-scale production playing to four and five thousand people at a time.

We toured bases in Alaska, the Philippines, and Japan, at Naples, Frankfurt, Berlin, and Guantanamo Bay, among others, filming wives telling their favorite stories about life on a military base or among a foreign and not always friendly population. We were looking for stories like the one I recall a young second lieutenant's wife telling on herself in Frankfurt. Her mischievous husband told her that all second lieutenants' wives had to snap to attention and salute the commanding officer when he drove by. So she did. At first the commanding officer tried to ignore her, but she finally got to him. One day he had his driver stop the car and asked her what she thought she was doing. She told him, he solemnly returned her salute, and officially released her from having to acknowledge him any more. Only when she rushed to tell her friends and saw them collapse with laughter did she realize that she had been thoroughly put on.

The stories that won the prize of an all-expense-paid trip back home, including tea with the First Lady at the White House, were often not as interesting as the off-the-record tales told me by the various officers. Nearly every post claimed the record for the stealing prowess of the local population. In Naples, for example, an executive officer solemnly described how a light cruiser in dry dock for refitting disappeared completely during a lunch-hour period. "His" Neapolitans, he informed me, not without a certain pride, had dismantled and stolen the entire warship in just under sixty minutes.

However, first prize would have to go to Clark Air Force Base's Filipinos, who for a time systematically looted the sprawling complex. The situation got so bad that the air force instituted an hourly helicopter patrol of the entire perimeter fence line. Nothing seemed to help until one evening an officer casually asked the just returned patrol pilot if all four gates were operating normally.

"How many gates?" the pilot asked.

"Four," replied the officer.

"Sorry, but there are five," the pilot assured him.

They stared at each other and the duty officer reached for the phone. The Filipinos, displaying the ingenuity that made the Japanese miserable during the occupation, had constructed a fifth gate complete with guardhouse, MPs checking trucks in and out, everything that would look normal from the air, while they relieved the base of tons of material.

Our Military Wife of the Year Award lasted for nine years. Although it had not the drama of celebrities entertaining combat troops, and consequently failed to get much exposure, it was nevertheless a most satisfying undertaking. It represents a classic case of a purely commercial enterprise developing into an altruistic event enjoyed by a lot of people. Because we were doing so well, the Harrell organization was talked about in the higher military circles, an ironic circumstance that helped commercially whether we liked it or not. Our competitors were never very pleased, and that may have contributed to the army's decision to withdraw its support, which because of interservice rivalry, made it impossible to proceed.

My involvement with the military has caused me more than once to reflect on the basic reason for its existence. It is a sad fact of life that we must spend huge sums of money keeping men and women under arms because we fear that without protection someone will destroy us. A fact is a fact, no matter how unpleasant, and since we must delegate the business of bearing arms to a relatively small number of our fellow citizens, I believe they should have our maximum support and trust.

Critics of our economic system tend to use the word *commercial* derogatorily, to imply exploitation. The fact is, the commercial process, like every other human endeavor, can be misused, but employed properly as a stimulant to and reward for our creative abilities, it results in a happier, easier, and fuller life for us all. My own professional experience illustrates my point.

Remember the Hula Hoop? Millions of people had a lot of fun and got some much needed exercise twirling that circular plastic band around various portions of their anatomies. I was one of the first to publicize and manufacture Hula Hoops and was myself a "hooper" of no small capability. Today someone would probably point out that psychologists endorse the Hoop as a tension-releasing therapeutic tool, but in the Hoop's heyday it was simply deemed good, clean, inexpensive fun.

Did you ever manage to guess which twin had the Toni? I pioneered that product on radio and television and I have yet to hear a woman (men didn't do that sort of thing in those days) complain of capitalistic exploitation because she could do her own hair at home for less.

And the Papermate pen. I was hired to show you that a revolution in the country's writing habits was at hand. I think we can say that the ballpoint pen has made writing more simple and convenient, and it may have increased contact between people. Now that's the kind of revolution I heartily endorse. Formula 409, plus what emerged from it, is merely another example of the positive results of commercial developments.

Chapter Seventeen

One thing I have not done during my life thus far is keep a diary. I have been much too busy making things happen to have time to record them. But Lois did and I have never once asked to see what she has written, nor, I must admit, has she offered to show me. Until very recently. She read the first chapters of this manuscript and volunteered the suggestion that she might be able to give some parts of it a little additional depth. She sorted through the pages of her diaries and selected some excerpts that she feels are appropriate. Here, in her own words, is how my wife viewed some of the significant decisions in our lives. The italics are mine, to give the reader a sense of chronology.

How we first met.

"Having a good time last night until the student body presi-

dent asked me to dance. His name is Art Linkletter. All the girls
were giggling and I think a bit jealous, but I think he's much
too conceited. In the middle of the dance he told me I didn't
know how to pivot. He said I was dancing too far away from
him. I couldn't wait for the dance to end. The nerve! I don't
know what everybody sees in him!"

A few days later.

"Art Linkletter called me today. I don't know how he got my
number but he called to ask me to the fraternity dance. Wow!
I couldn't tell him that I'm not allowed to go because mother
thinks that's not the place for a respectable girl so I told him
mother doesn't approve of me going out with someone she
doesn't know. He said, 'Well, let's take care of that right now.
Put her on the phone.' When mother picked up the phone I
thought my date was off for sure. I couldn't believe it when she
said afterward that he seemed like a nice boy and that if I went
with *him* she wouldn't mind. She hasn't even met him!"

She pivoted just fine at the frat house. Then, some time later.

"Art asked me to marry him. We've been going together long
enough so I'm sure. I was sure a long time ago. We talked about
his career and having a family and agreed that we would always
put our relationship first. We both want children but he senses
that he is really going to go somewhere and I think so too. So
when the time comes and I have to make a choice, I will stay
with him as much as possible. The children will come and go
but we want to look past that and enjoy life when the family is
gone. Strange to think that far ahead but we are both that way.
Too many people sacrifice everything for their children and lose
one another while they're doing it. Hope we're right."

Many years later.

"Only Sharon and Diane at home now. I've been reading way back [*in the diaries*] and I know now that we have done the right thing. Art's career has gotten bigger than even he dreamed and I've had to go with him all around the world. I love the children and would never leave them with someone I could not trust completely. But I love my husband and might not have kept him had I not been willing to be with him. Now, with only two at home with us it's simpler. It looks as though we're all going to have to learn to ski! Thanks to Lowell Thomas. The girls are looking forward to it."

But when Lois got the hang of skiing she became as enthusiastic as I am. She stays right with me too, the way she has all along our exciting, challenging life journey. We have always discussed our dreams and plans with my knowing the feeling of security that comes when a woman is always there to give a man a base and in times of stress to protect his emotional flank. And she continues to do this, even though I have gradually changed the professional emphasis of the second half of my life.

It is difficult for most of us to think past our own lifetimes. It is easy to theorize about the future ten, twenty, or fifty years from now, but to sit down and face the reality that I may not be a part of those times gives me pause. Some people regard this life as merely a preparation for the next, and they, in many ways, are the fortunate ones. Few doubts and supposedly no fears plague them as they cross the threshold and rush eagerly to the rewards of an afterlife. From time to time some even hurry the process, believing that dying for a Christian cause gives them extra points in the great final computation.

For my own part, as I've pointed out from time to time in these chapters, God's hand was upon me well before I was capable of even sensing His presence. My ability to communicate is, I believe, a God-given gift. At the risk of sounding presumptions while thinking of what lies around the next turn. The terms *good vibes* and *bad vibes* are used much too loosely these days, but the vibrations I feel from the silent response of the people in front of me act as very real guidelines as to how I will approach that next discursive turn in the road.

The unspoken rapport between myself and an audience becomes a thrilling experience, one I could never have if I did not always speak extemporaneously. The audience, projecting its vibes, actually leads me through the course of my speech. Time and again people compliment me on the thoroughness of my preparation and on the fact that I must have taken great pains to learn the subtle nuances that had me relate so closely to that particular group. The truth, at once gratifying and humbling, is that I relied on thirty-five years of professional experience to keep my cool and on a God-given ability to pluck emotional input out of thin air and translate it into a meaningful experience for all concerned.

My role as a communicator has grown steadily (as a sample page from my weekly itinerary shows) since I stopped appearing regularly on television. I am now, as the popular phrase would have it, getting it all together in a role that I find immensely fulfilling. The results of years of experience, insight, and acquired knowledge now enable me not only to entertain but also to provoke audiences to thought and, I hope, leave them a little richer for the encounter.

If all this sounds like the culmination of a successful career, it is. Yet it's not. Rather, one career has led to another that promises in many ways to be even more rewarding than the first. I'm not through winning in the sense of using my professional expertise to hold an audience. That remains a supreme thrill for me, one I savor with a deep humility that acknowledges God's role in this great adventure. No man could ask for more.

tuous, I do not see how any Christian can fail to acknowledge and be appreciative of the obvious fact that the hand guiding the universe represents something beyond our conscious awareness, and that the same hand bestows on all of us particular gifts and then aids us in developing them. Those of us who heed Him, function as successful Christians; those who do not, sooner or later fall by the wayside.

I mentioned feeling His presence comforting me at Los Angeles International Airport right after Diane's death; that was a specific, almost physical sensation. On a much broader scale, however, my very success opened my eyes to the astonishing information that I may well have been guided all along this Christian journey. When I was first really "hot," as we say in show business, all doors were open to me and I walked through most of them. I worked in motion pictures, acted on the stage, played nightclubs, appeared in television dramas; I could do all those things because my name assured an automatic box-office draw to any producer or promoter. I tried them all and was uncomfortable with most of them.

Inevitably I returned to television, radio, and personal appearances in the role that I knew and liked best, relying on my ability to speak and to communicate with anyone on whatever level. I began to realize that had I tried from the beginning to make my way in any of the other entertainment forms, the odds were great that I would have failed. Who or what kept steering me along the proper path? Only a fool or an atheist would deny the existence of a power beyond ourselves.

For some, God's guidance acts like a cast around their broken spirit, a steadying influence that takes them safely through troubled times. In my case, I feel a power beyond myself every time I stand to speak in front of an audience. I've written in these pages about being able to "read" an audience, but there is something more going on between the listeners and me. As I speak, my thoughts are racing ahead, much as a driver's do when he finds himself guiding his car merely by going through the mo-